Hockney Paints the Stage

Hockney Paints the Stage

by Martin Friedman

with contributions by
John Cox, John Dexter, David Hockney
and Stephen Spender

Hayward Gallery, London
1 August to 29 September 1985

Arts Council of Great Britain

London exhibition presented by the Arts Council
and sponsored by **Honeywell**

The Arts Council would like to express its
gratitude to David Hockney and to Martin
Friedman and his staff at the Walker Art Center,
Minneapolis, where the exhibition originated.

First published in Great Britain in 1983 by Thames and
Hudson Ltd, London

This edition published by the Arts Council of Great Britain,
1985

First published in the U.S.A. by Walker Art Center
and Abbeville Press

Dimensions are in inches, height precedes width
precedes depth.

All works collection the artist unless noted otherwise.

ISBN O 7287 0447 1

(cover, chosen by David Hockney for the Arts Council showing of
Hockney Paints the Stage) detail, large-scale painted environment
based on Hockney's design for Poulenc's opera *Les Mamelles de
Tirésias* 1983 (See pp 216, 217 for overall view)

(frontispiece)
Les Mamelles de Tirésias 1980
oil on canvas
36 x 48
Courtesy Galerie Alice Pauli

Contents

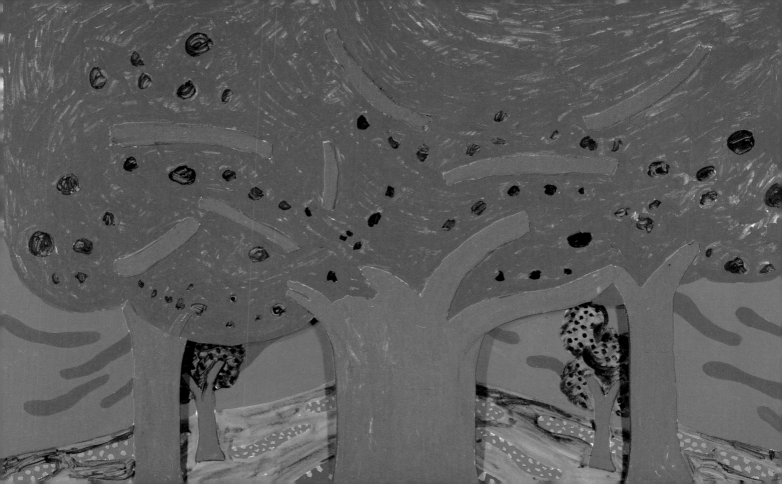

Painting into Theater

Martin Friedman

England in the mid-1960s was experiencing unprecedented euphoria as British reserve gave way to Dionysian revel. In addition to such earthshaking contributions to popular culture as the Beatles and Carnaby Street fashion, London was the scene of a high-voltage, gleefully anti-establishment revolution in the visual arts. From such once-venerable strongholds of academicism as the Royal College of Art, the Slade School and St. Martin's, an army of shaggy young painters and sculptors suddenly emerged to become instant celebrities of the art world and lively new galleries vied to present their exuberant creations to an international audience.

Of this talented crop, certainly the most media-genic was the young Yorkshireman, David Hockney, barely graduated from the Royal College. An engaging enfant terrible, he made his entry into the bubbling art scene with a brilliant job of self-presentation. Though he had begun art school as a rather conventionally-attired student, by the time he graduated, his dark hair had metamorphosed into a blond corona and his flamboyant wardrobe included a gold lamé jacket. The theatrics of the 60s encouraged style and invention, qualities the young artist from the industrial town of Bradford had in large supply.

His paintings of this period, bold in scale, color and theme, were a felicitous melange of figurative and abstract forms, ranging from surreal landscapes and interiors to factual ink and brush portraits. His fantasy world was inhabited by magicians, hypnotists, actors, nudes, elephants, snakes and monster-like personages. Anonymous in feature and stance, many Hockney figures, even in this early phase, were characters in enigmatic little dramas. The box-like interiors, in which such scenes were played by male and female nudes, seemingly in a state of catatonia, were quotations from the sardonic imagery of his fellow Englishman, Francis Bacon, whose work Hockney still admires.

Abstract expressionist and Pop sensibilities collided head-on in Hockney's early canvases and, materializing through a network of heavy de Kooningesque brushstrokes, blobs, daubs and spatters of spontaneously applied color became

The Garden
drawing for *L'Enfant et les Sortilèges* 1980
gouache on foam core and paper
26 × 40

7

8

schematized clouds, doorways, rainbows, furniture, numerals and lettering. No effort was made to be specific: interiors became panoramas, figures dissolved into landscapes. The common denominator of those paintings was their border-line reality. Such images developed intuitively; they seem to have floated onto the canvas from a dream. Indeed, the grimacing phantoms in Hockney's paintings and drawings of the late 1950s and early 1960s might be regarded as an ongoing series of demonic self-portraits in which a conventionally-brought-up English lad delighted in placing himself at the center of slightly menacing paradoxical situations. There is a touch of the morality play here. Many of the bizarre characters inhabiting Hockney's paintings, prints and illustrations for folktales and poems throughout the 1960s were at once sardonic and ingenuous objectifications of such foibles as malice, greed, pomposity and licentiousness.

A decade later, this primitivistic imagery would give way to an ultra-refined expression of crystalline contours. Then after assiduously pursuing this new direction, Hockney in the late 1970s would again reverse himself, shattering his laboriously-achieved perfection to return with abandon to more intuitive painting.

Such vacillation between stylistic poles has always characterized Hockney's art. Equally typical has been his eagerness to explore new areas beyond painting, drawing and printmaking. In 1966, his work moved tentatively into the world of three dimensions when he designed sets and costumes for Alfred Jarry's *Ubu Roi* at the Royal Court Theatre in London. But it was his vivid conceptions for the Glyndebourne Festival and the Metropolitan Opera that made stage design so integral to his artistic vision. While his theater design grew out of earlier painting themes, it eventually became a source of new motifs and stylistic approaches that found their way back to the studio. Indeed, as a consequence of his immersion in theater projects, Hockney's painting has taken energetic new directions.

How did Hockney's involvement with theater begin, and how, particularly, did an artist once so prominently identified with Pop-related imagery find himself not only in the midst of an alien art form—grand opera—but, from his new vantage, exerting strong influence on its presentation? His devotion to the stage was no sudden conversion, but reflected a long-time interest in music and theater that had begun during his Bradford Grammar School days. As he points out, no English schoolboy can escape an early introduction to the theater.

Every term you study a Shakespeare play thoroughly, which means you study fifteen plays in the years you are in school. I know a number quite well, though I can't remember vast chunks by heart. At school, if you were a wicked little boy, which I was, the punishment given out by the teachers was to write out all the classical allusions listed in the back of the Shakespeare book you were studying, so I know a lot of them—I'll tell you—because I had to do that often. That was a lot worse than writing out lines saying, "I must not break any

Man in a Museum (or You're in the Wrong Movie)   1962
oil on canvas
69 × 60
Collection The British Council

windows today," fifty times, because any inventive schoolboy will think of ways of doing that easily, like using five pens at once.

On a less academic level, theater and music were always part of his life. He had no formal musical training and claims no special expertise. Rather, his exposure was limited to whatever orchestras or musical productions might have come through town. During his youth, he wistfully recalls, there were three theaters in Bradford and, eight miles away in Leeds, were another six or seven.

As a child, I went to the theater a great deal. My father took me every Saturday to the Bradford Alhambra to see whatever was on. Most of the time, it was simply a variety show. The first opera I ever saw was when my father took me there to see the Carl Rosa Opera Company doing La Bohème. *I loved it. I thought it was a marvelous spectacle. I'm sure it was tacky, really, but you know, to a ten-year-old boy it looked unbelievably lavish, and the music was better than you'd normally hear in the theater. It certainly sounded better than the regular orchestra they had there, which would have been called a quintet anywhere else. In the late 1940s, every week there was something different at the theater, and it was full every night. That was pre-television, of course. Only when I moved to London did I see first-class productions.*

From the age of ten to the age of twenty, during the concert season in Bradford, I went two or three times a week, usually to hear the Hallé Orchestra or the Yorkshire Symphony Orchestra. During all my years at grammar school and art school in Bradford, I went to every concert I could. We didn't have a Gramophone at home. You could listen to the BBC at times, but there were seven of us in the house and it wasn't easy to get to listen to music there.

Though Hockney had made the transition effortlessly from the Royal College to London's art world, his flair for self-promotion was equalled by a distinctive artistic sensibility that was quickly recognized by fellow artists and critics. He could draw superbly, his vision was fresh and provocative, he was an avid experimenter, and his output was prodigious as he explored many themes and media. His subjects ranged widely, from nursery tales to intimate explorations of sexuality.

In 1966 Hockney was invited by Ian Cuthbertson of London's Royal Court Theatre to design sets and costumes for Alfred Jarry's *Ubu Roi*. Given his penchant for depicting down-and-out denizens of marginal worlds, he was an inspired choice for this icon of dislocated reality. Jarry's absurdist play, with its mock histrionics and potshots at institutions and mores, was well served by Hockney's quasi-cartoon style. The result was a series of drawings of *Ubu Roi*'s "blissed-out" dramatis personae bumbling from one demented situation to another. Reflecting on his designs for *Ubu Roi*, Hockney says the transition from studio to stage posed no difficulties.

I had played with those ideas before and thought of all my pictures as drama. Even the way I was painting at that time was a kind of theatrical exaggeration.

Seated Woman Drinking Tea,
Being Served by a Standing Companion   1963
oil on canvas
78 × 84
Abrams Family Collection

11

With its rudimentary sets and costumes that turned the actors into walking assemblage sculptures, Hockney's *Ubu Roi* was a droll variation on the then current *arte povera* style. His drawings were translated by the Royal Court's scene painters into painted backdrops, each approximately 8 by 21 feet, and to his amazement, every nuance—even erasures and corrections—was enlarged. Working on *Ubu Roi* was novel and challenging for Hockney. As the production took shape, he added new props and set elements. Following Jarry's stage directions, he decided that large, crudely drawn lettering would define each scene—Ubu's Banquet Room, Ubu's Closet, The Polish Army. Similar lettering would appear years later in the form of giant alphabet blocks spelling each composer's name in the Metropolitan Opera's production of *Parade*.

Though Hockney's designs for *Ubu Roi* attracted favorable critical response, mainly from the visual arts establishment, his approach did not adapt readily to the needs of most theater companies. There were no immediate invitations to take on new commissions and not for eight years did he have another chance to function in this tantalizing sphere. In 1974, the Glyndebourne Festival Opera, outside London, commissioned him to design sets and costumes for Stravinsky's *The Rake's Progress*. The result was a brilliant, highly contemporary variation on the crosshatched engraving style of William Hogarth. Enthusiastic public and critical reaction to his first operatic venture led to a second Glyndebourne commission: in 1978, he turned his talents to *The Magic Flute*, Mozart's fanciful re-creation of ancient Egypt. Both operas were directed by John Cox who, from the start, had spotted the theatrical possibilities in Hockney's idiosyncratic imagery.

In 1974, while living in Paris, Hockney had another opportunity to think about the stage. He had just completed *The Rake's Progress* designs when Roland Petit asked him to design a set for the Ballet de Marseilles. The ballet, *Septentrion*, a new work with libretto by Yves Novarre and music by Marius Constant, required a painted backdrop depicting a swimming pool in the south of France. "I was not thinking in space when I did the drawing," Hockney recalls, nor was he involved in any production decisions. His design, an enlargement of a crayon sketch, contained four major areas: a house, a courtyard with topiary, a swimming pool and a blue Mediterranean sky against which appears a Léger-like sculpture in the form of a polychrome sunburst.

Not until 1979 did Hockney again undertake another large-scale theatrical commission. The transplanted Englishman John Dexter, who in 1974 became production supervisor at the Metropolitan Opera in New York, invited the painter to join him in creating an evening of 20th-century French musical theater, that would consist of three works spawned during World War I: the ballet, *Parade*, by Erik Satie, *Les Mamelles de Tirésias* by Francis Poulenc, and Maurice Ravel's *L'Enfant et les Sortilèges*. *Parade*, as the evening soon became known, was widely praised, with reaction exceeding anything the Met had

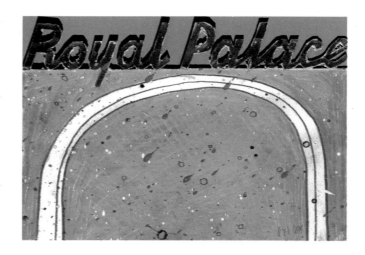

Cave
drawing for *Ubu Roi*   1966
crayon, pencil on paper
6 × 8¼

Royal Palace
drawing for *Ubu Roi*   1966
crayon, pencil, metallic crayon, gouache on folded,
cut-out cardboard
8 × 8

Ur Curtain
drawing for *Ubu Roi*   1966
crayon, pencil on paper
15 × 20

Collection The Museum of Modern Art, New York
Gift of John Kasmin

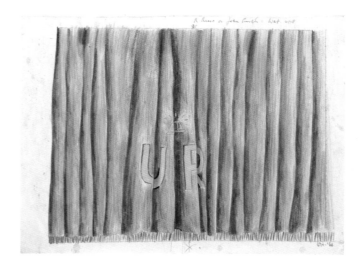

Ordinary Picture   1964
acrylic on canvas
72 × 72
Collection Hirshhorn Museum and Sculpture Garden,
Smithsonian Institution

Detail of *drawing for the Design for Roland Petit's
Ballet, Septentrion*   1975
crayon on paper
14 × 17
Collection Jean Léger

anticipated. This factor, plus the inspiration of working together, prompted the Dexter/Hockney team to take on another triple bill a year later devoted to works by a single composer, Igor Stravinsky. Again, a ballet led the program—Stravinsky's celebrated evocation of a fertility rite, *Le Sacre du Printemps*. This was followed by the lyrical *Le Rossignol*, based on Hans Christian Andersen's tale, *The Nightingale*, and the concluding piece was the opera-oratorio *Oedipus Rex*, with a libretto by Jean Cocteau.

The constant compromise required in designing for the theater has dissuaded many artists from taking on such demanding projects over which they ultimately have little control. Though conscious of these pitfalls, Hockney has been unable to resist the seductive, glittering realm of the stage, demonstrating a willingness to adapt to its special demands.

The theater is an area where you're forced to be and do certain things. First of all, you work from literary sources, and in opera you have to be true to the music. The theater world tends to think that a strong artist won't cooperate enough—that he's not used to such an approach and tends to do things his own way, and other people simply have to fit in with this. It's true when you're painting a picture you don't really have to defer to anybody, whereas in the theater, you do. On the other hand, although I understand the need to listen to someone else's ideas in the theater, I'm not going to do something that goes against what I think should be there.

If Hockney occasionally begrudges the time the theater takes from his painting, once caught up in a production he is virtually addicted to its realization and involves himself in every detail, with suggestions for staging as well as design. While responsive to an opera's directorial and musical requirements, when it comes to actual execution of his design, he does not readily relinquish authority. He is obsessed with details and carrying an idea through to completion. For example, though a costume sketch might consist of a few rudimentary lines and color washes, he knows how the finished costume should look.

If I want some special detail, I find the best person technically who can do the work. I wouldn't turn the job over to just anyone who says the costume could be made this or that way. Everything could be destroyed if I did that!

True to his word, at Glyndebourne he oversaw the fabrication of a mythological menagerie, featuring the fire-spitting dragon that greets the noble Prince Tamino in *The Magic Flute*'s opening forest scene. Though these wondrous creatures were fabricated by the theater's technical shops, and some sewing on them was done by the local ladies, Hockney reserved for himself the enjoyable tasks of painting and otherwise embellishing the surfaces of these beasts. A more recent instance of attention to a costume's finish was the resolution of the cat situation in Ravel's *L'Enfant et les Sortilèges*. He decided the amorous pair of felines, one white, the other black, had to be absolutely correct in all details of features and fur, and to insure this, he sought out one Rostislav Doboujinsky, a Parisian wizard of such marvels.

1

2

3

4

Thanks to this wise, if costly, decision, the eyes and fur of the purring, yowling beasts glisten convincingly under the Met's lights.

Such concern with all facets of a production and a capacity for collaborating with fellow creative spirits have been crucial to Hockney's success as a designer. Equally important has been an ability to draw upon his rich store of imagery, much of which first appeared in his paintings during the early 1960s. A recognizable vocabulary of symbols characterizes his art. These distinctive Hockney leitmotifs, chimerically assume various meanings as their contexts change. Both borrowed and invented forms, they derive from his travels, from art history, and from his immediate surroundings.

Some distinction should be made between the subject matter Hockney favors and specific design motifs that are components of these. His subject matter covers many categories; it includes figures, objects and landscapes, as well as intricate combinations thereof. His motifs are the building blocks of his art. For example, he has a specific way of representing rippling water in a few wavy lines; he represents rain in a few diagonals; his puffy clouds and bulky tree shapes are instantly identifiable.

These motifs have many sources. Some echo solid architectural forms such as pyramids and stairways, others are based on ephemera such as sunlight on water or the arc of a rainbow. They are his personal hieroglyphs. This visual syntax accumulated as basic forms underwent permutations easily traceable from one work to another. Themes that made their debuts in the 1960s resonate through his production.

Hockney did not deliberately set out to create an iconography. Many distinctive forms in his work have their origins in casual sketches and not in some mystical search for inner meanings. He regards himself mainly as an illustrator, not a symbol-maker. He deals with recognizable forms— whatever distortions they may undergo in the painting process. His perception of his work, however, does not preclude the possibility that his use of factual description can on occasion have symbolic portent. When Hockney first started making illustrations, they were vehicles for his subjective feelings about literary and poetic ideas. Accordingly, subject matter, filtered through his own experience, was drastically transformed. In illustrating a poem or story he cared less about describing it in every detail than about producing his version of the subject. In the 1960s, he recalls, the notion of a young artist referring to his work as illustration—despite the growing attraction of Pop Art for his generation—had a certain opprobrium about it.

In the mid-60s, many people thought art had nothing whatsoever to do with illustration, and often if you used the word it was meant as a "put-down." Yet I knew perfectly well that many great things are illustrative. Rembrandt's Bible illustrations, for example. Hogarth was, of course, a great illustrator. What about Bruegel, Goya and Daumier? I deliberately annoyed many people by insisting that a lot of great art is illustration. There are those lines of Auden. "To me art's subject is the human clay, / And landscape but a background to a

Details from (1) *California Art Collector*, (2) *Iowa*, (3) *Les Mamelles de Tirésias*, (4) *Hollywood Hills House*. (These works are reproduced in their entirety elsewhere.)

torso; / *All Cézanne's apples I would give away / For one small Goya or a Daumier.*" When I came across those lines in Letter to Lord Byron, I liked them. Of course, Cézanne's apples are wonderful, but Auden was really taking a dig at Roger Fry, for whom "significant form" was everything, and who thought the illustrative side of art was nothing at all.

In this spirit, Hockney applied his fine descriptive line to etchings, lithographs and aquatints while continuing to turn out large, splashy, figurative paintings. In contrast to the strong color and bravura technique of the paintings, his graphic works were more introspective in theme and approach, full of closely-observed as well as invented shapes. They were Hockney's image banks, proliferating with numerous motifs that would appear in more dramatic fashion in his paintings and theater sets.

Hockney's determination to make art out of illustration places his work somewhere between Pop Art, whose subject matter comes from the everyday world, and the long-established descriptive tradition in British painting. At the Royal College he had experienced the exhilarating effects of Pop, subscribing to its rejection of pure abstraction in favor of subjects drawn from the immediate world. Another early formative influence was the spiky, aggressive figuration of Jean Dubuffet, the great French *maître* of anti-culture. In fact, the leading character in Hockney's little dramas on paper and canvas during the early 1960s was a large-headed, totemistic being, decidedly reminiscent of Dubuffet's irascible *art-brut* dwarf who gleefully spat in the eye of convention.

The juxtaposition of unrelated forms has always fascinated Hockney. In this respect, his work is close to that of the American "popsters," Oldenburg, Lichtenstein and Dine, through whose distinctive styles objects from the real world assume startling new identities. Like them, Hockney envisaged an ambiguous realm where reality is constantly subverted. In this world, logic and irrationality are indistinguishable; it is a world of the mind, a surreal place of constantly shifting meanings. Each artist has charted its mysterious terrain through personal symbols. Anthropomorphism is the core of Oldenburg's elaborate iconography, replete with provocative variations on electric plugs, typewriter erasers and clothespins which, in his view, are metaphors for the human body. Dine describes his well-known hearts, robes and gates as surrogates for his emotions; these are undergoing convulsive variations in his increasingly expressionistic paintings, drawings and prints. Less humanistic is Lichtenstein's iconography, a stylized compendium of style itself. In his paintings a wide variety of subjects—still-life arrangements à la Picasso, comic-strip characters, classical friezes—are reduced to posteresque areas of "commercial art" color bordered by black lines.

How does Hockney's symbolism relate to the object-oriented work of the Americans? While he shares their interest in using everyday forms in his paintings, these are rarely portrayed as single images but as elements in

Great Pyramid at Giza with Broken Head from Thebes   1963
oil on canvas
72 × 72
Private collection

18

19

A Grand Procession of Dignitaries
Painted in the Semi-Egyptian Style   1961
oil on canvas
84 × 144
Collection Edwin Janss

complex interiors and landscapes. Thus, psychologically and aesthetically, his symbology is more diffuse than the Americans'.

Though Hockney's search for subject matter seems endless, certain favorite themes undergo frequent recycling, turning up afresh in paintings, prints and stage set designs. Among these reliables: human figures, sometimes rendered with anatomical accuracy, other times appearing as robot-like beings; animals, including lizards, leopards and fantastic beasts reminiscent of medieval heraldry; landscape forms, including many kinds of trees, from wispy palms to bulky oaks, as well as clouds and rainbows; fire and water; domestic objects, including flower-patterned upholstered chairs, coffee tables, lamps, drapes, vases of flowers, doors and windows, and "fine art objects" such as paintings and sculptures. A typical Hockney subject, water, will undergo many variations. He is interested in its transparent and reflective properties. In his well-known swimming pool paintings, light reflects on its surface and people and objects seen through it are magnified and distorted. Nor is he content to allow water to remain still in his paintings. In them it appears as rain, it sprays from showerheads, it spurts from sprinklers on green California lawns, and in his theater design for *The Magic Flute*, manifests itself on a grand scale as a waterfall.

A cursory review of Hockney's painting up to the mid-1970s reveals at least four general subjects that have affected his stage design. The first and most prophetic, the theater theme, complete with actor and curtain, first appeared in his drawings and paintings of the early 1960s. Another important infusion is Egyptian-inspired subject matter, such as pyramids, great stone sculptures and figures drawn in profile. Third, Hockney makes frequent reference to "modern art" styles, freely utilizing Fauve and cubist techniques in his paintings. Finally, the color, light and sybaritic lifestyle of California have measurably affected his painting, particularly in such themes as swimming pools, house interiors and landscapes. These subject areas have a way of invading one another in Hockney's paintings. For example, one of his early pageants in paint, the large 1961 phantasmagoria called *A Grand Procession of Dignitaries Painted in the Semi-Egyptian Style*, combines theater and Egyptian motifs. Featuring three standing figures, sumptuously attired in a melange of modes, this picture, he says, was made at a time when he was just becoming interested in theatrical effects. At the top is a rudimentary curtain indicated in a few sketchy lines. The "semi-Egyptian style" refers to the flat, diagrammatic representation of its figures, rendered in profile, a manner reminiscent of ancient Egyptian wall painting. The middle figure's head is a direct takeoff on Egyptian tomb painting technique. Hockney discusses the genesis of this carnival-like work.

I bought a large canvas, before I went to America, from an art student who couldn't afford to paint on it. Then I grabbed the largest space I could find at the Royal College of Art. I thought, my God, this canvas is so big, I must paint a

Still Life with Figure and Curtain   1963
oil on canvas
78 × 84
Private collection

Two Men in a Shower   1963
oil on canvas
60 × 60
Private collection

big scene. The idea for it came from the 1904 poem by <u>Constantine Cavafy</u> called <u>Waiting for the Barbarians</u>. It's one of his greatest poems. There are those ironic lines about people dressing up to impress others. I painted the figures to look like cutouts—inside each huge costume you can see the outline of a small person trying to look bigger and more important.

Such reduction of characters to simple Brechtian stereotypes—here, the general, the bishop, the businessman—occurs in many Hockney works of this period. The cartooned performers in *A Grand Procession of Dignitaries* anticipate the cheerful eccentrics who inhabit the 1966 *Ubu Roi* drawings.

In Hockney's theater paintings, what action there is takes place in a <u>box</u>-like enclosure. Though he used frontal, or one-point perspective to define the walls that contain these little events, their settings, nevertheless, are ambiguous. They take place in some no-man's-land between reality and theatrical illusion. In using the stage metaphor, fact and fantasy dissolve into one another, and ordinary events take on mythic connotations.

In the 1960s theater paintings, perspective is constantly modified, if not altogether disregarded. Though the stage's back wall parallels the picture surface, what goes on in its shallow volume has little to do with how things are perceived. Frequently, objects float in space and, perversely, parallel lines do not converge, but diverge, as they recede.

In the 1963 *Still Life with Figure and Curtain*, a faceless androgyne stands before an elaborate fleur-de-lis tapestry—at its feet a still life of flowers and fruit. The curtain and still life are more "real" than the figure which, composed of a few cylindrical forms, is far more abstract than any de Chirico dummy. But such impersonal quality, Hockney says, was precisely what he had in mind.

I had no desire to paint a personality because the curtain was the most important thing. I wanted a pattern on it and stenciled on the design. If I'd painted the figure with personality, it would have become the focus. So, I thought, I'll reduce it to a simple form, an old-fashioned skittle or bowling pin. In those days, you still had them in pubs.

So important was that fleur-de-lis curtain to Hockney that in the 1980 *Les Mamelles de Tirésias* set, he virtually reproduced it in all its detail. In front of its monumental reincarnation, a top-hatted impresario introduced the program for the evening.

Hockney's curtain was not limited to theatrical subjects but also appears in many of his domestic interiors, which he regards as another form of theater. In those interiors, it assumes many variations, from window drapery overrun with tropical foliage to shower curtains. The fleur-de-lis, in simplified form, adorns the drape behind the nudes in the 1963 *Seated Woman Drinking Tea, Being Served by a Standing Companion*. The plastic bathroom curtain in *Two Men in a Shower*, also from that year, is enlivened with birds and starfish silhouettes. We are not certain if we are looking at a stage set or a living room in *Two Friends and Two Curtains*, 1963. Behind the patterned drapes in

23

this painting loom two large, stone heads, one in profile, the other full-face, that fuse into one another.

Surely one of Hockney's most cryptic curtain-bordered stage paintings is *The Hypnotist*, also from 1963, in which a menacing, dark-suited character, described in profile, stands in front of his own white shadow. This composition, quite an active one by Hockney's standards, is also the subject of an etching and aquatint, in which the exchange of energy between hypnotist and subject is even more pronounced. From the point where their hands converge, leaps a white zig-zag of "electricity," striking an armless robotic type at the other end of the stage. Neatly lettered on the dark border at the bottom of the painting is *The Hypnotist*.

A particularly ambitious treatment of the curtain that even more clearly anticipates the artist's interest in theater design occurs in two paintings starring Hockney's London dealer, John Kasmin. One of these, *Play within a Play*, 1963, has Kasmin pressing his hands and nose against a sheet of clear plastic, like a man pushing against a shop window to look inside. Except for a narrow strip of flooring, the background is a tasseled curtain adorned with a peculiar pastoral featuring several vaguely Egyptian figures, a tree and rainbow. This enigmatic work, Hockney explains, had its origin in a museum.

This is how Play within a Play *was done. I went to the National Gallery one day and found they'd just put up several paintings by Domenichino containing depictions of curtains. In those days, I used to go to the National at least twice a week, getting to know the pictures, and when I saw this brand new room, I was quite excited. Although I didn't think these were great pictures, they had a quality of tapestry, which was an illusion. I suddenly was aware of many levels of illusion. In one of the paintings the corner of a curtain was pulled away, and standing there was a dwarf. It was like taking a layer of the painting and peeling it back, and there would be another and another . . . I decided to paint a curtain that would look like a tapestry. Then I took photographs of Kasmin pressed against the glass door of his gallery; from these I painted him on a sheet of plastic and put it in front of the picture. He looks as if he were trapped within the shallow space of the picture.*

Another example of Hockney's preoccupation with theater is the 1963 *Closing Scene*, in which a white curtain, outlined in black on a primed canvas, is parted slightly by a costumed performer to reveal an opulent landscape. Discussing this picture, Hockney reflects on the visual and psychological relationship of the theater curtain to the artist's canvas.

If you take the painting off its stretcher, it is like a curtain. When you paint a curtain on canvas, the illusion is that it's an inch deep at most. If you paint a curtain pulled back, it reveals a picture, as a stage curtain does in the theater. A curtain in a painting always does that, even if it's on a window. The little event you see in the vertical strip in Closing Scene *was based on a Persian miniature in the Victoria and Albert Museum which I got to know quite well. The Royal College of Art painting school is in the same building. I was always*

Play within a Play 1963
tapestry
72 × 78

(opposite)
The Actor   1964
acrylic on canvas
65½ × 65½
Collection Mr. and Mrs. Eugene Rosenberg

Closing Scene   1963
oil on canvas
47 × 47
Private collection

wandering through different sections of the museum on my way to the cafeteria for tea. That's how I got to know the collection.

The curtain motif continued throughout paintings and drawings of the 1960s and 70s, sometimes with clear references to the theater, other times in undefined settings. The interior represented in a 1964 painting, *The Actor,* could be either a stage or a living room. In it, a large-headed figure, whose features are reminiscent of Egyptian sculpture, is unaccountably suspended in space. Sharing a dais with the actor are a couch, a cubistic potted plant, a pillow and an amorphous shape resembling a miniature mountain. In some paintings the curtain takes on strange solidity, especially when Hockney paints drapery folds as heavy tubular forms. The curtain in the 1964 *Cubist Boy with Colourful Tree* is rendered similarly to the solitary palm behind it—with raw modeling and no effort at nuance. The style of the gesturing boy is a not-so-subtle allusion to Cubism's early "primitive" phase.

So many references to the stage abound in Hockney's paintings that his eventual involvement with it, beginning with his work at the Royal Court Theatre, should have surprised no one. Yet his interest in theatrical themes was not limited to subject matter—it had a formal basis as well. By using theatrical metaphors in his paintings he felt freer to expand and contract space. Like his occasional subject, the magician, he has always delighted in paradoxical situations. In his theater scenes and interiors the rules of gravity and perspective were suspended as he turned volumes into planes, commanded disembodied heads to hover in space, and performed other wondrous feats. Yet such events, through Hockney's beguiling form and color, become an easily accepted new reality.

Though not as directly as the theater themes, other important categories of Hockney's subject matter have influenced his stage designs. The Egyptian syndrome is a fine example, including as it does numerous motifs that are mainstays in his work. He had improvised in such themes well before visiting that ancient land and learned about its stately art through books and frequent visits to the British Museum. During those few weeks abroad he made drawings of everything that interested him—not only the monumental vestiges of antiquity, but of present-day life in cities and villages. But always, his impressions of Egypt's fabled ruins were tempered by oblique commentary. Though captivated by the noble detritus of the pharaonic past, he could not help seeing Egypt in contemporary terms. Its scruffy palms, crowded streets, Shell station signs, villagers in flowing djellabas, camera-toting tourists, and ornate hotel rooms were as fascinating to him as the sphinx or the pyramids. Indeed, so intrigued was Hockney with Egypt that he would return in 1978. In the time-dislocating, atmospheric studies made during both visits, ancient and present-day Egypt coexist on the same level of consciousness. Despite the deprecations of harshly imposed modernity, the spirit of ancient Egypt was still detectable. Its great artistic styles, he recalls, had not lost their attraction.

Cubist Boy with Colourful Tree 1964
acrylic on canvas
65½ × 65½
Collection Hirshhorn Museum and Sculpture Garden,
Smithsonian Institution

I became interested in the Egyptian style, because it was a rigid art form with strict rules. Those rules had to be obeyed, so much so that the individual mark wasn't left. In fact, you never know who did what. This might not be the case exactly, but I loved the idea of the slightly anonymous style that everybody worked in.

The atmosphere of that country permeated his art. But though he incorporated its ancient forms in his painting, he never fell victim to the blandishments of historicism, preferring to take only what he needed from such awesome sources.

Especially interesting is the Egyptian flavor of his 1960s paintings of seated figures in box-like interiors. While compositionally these are variations on his theater pictures, they have their own quality. In *The Second Marriage*, painted in 1963, an unlikely couple—a sinister-looking man in dark glasses and business suit—and a cone-breasted lady in a white gown who vaguely resembles an ancient Egyptian deity—sit side by side on a couch. To the left of the man's head is painted the numeral 1; to the right of the bride's head, the numeral 2. On the spindly low table before this grim pair are a bottle of champagne and two glasses. Here, Hockney used a "shaped canvas"—he has cut its upper left and lower right edges of the painting to create the illusion of a three-dimensional cube. The "exterior" wall of the room is covered with flowered wallpaper; the front wall and ceiling have been "removed" so we can look in. A pair of patterned window drapes are in the background.

The Second Marriage, a brilliant exercise in spatial and stylistic contradiction, is about volume and flatness. Above all, it is about theatrics. Asked about the content of this odd vignette, Hockney discusses its occupants in formal terms and does not speculate on any emotional relationship that might exist between them. Indeed, for all the painting's elaborate detail, he says, it is not an illustration of a particular event. Instead, it is a cryptic, unresolved situation, and its interpretation is up to us.

These are very stylized figures. The woman's head is painted from a black and white photograph of the head of an Egyptian sculpture. They're just two different people—inventions of mine—and they seem to be made of different materials.

Such incongruity is the rule, not the exception, in his work. The exuberantly realized *The First Marriage*, 1962, reveals his delight in the felicitous union of completely unrelated styles.

The subtitle of both paintings is A Marriage of Styles. *I liked the idea of jumbling several styles within a single picture. It was like working with collage and I could add new meaning to it. One of the styles in these pictures happens to be Egyptian. The composition I used for both works was based on something I saw in a museum. Down a corridor, a friend of mine was standing next to an Egyptian wood figure. He was not looking at it but at something else—yet, for a moment, they looked connected, as though a man and wife had sat down together. I was amused by the idea and back at the hotel made a drawing from*

The First Marriage (A Marriage of Styles I) 1962
oil on canvas
72 × 60
Collection Tate Gallery

California Art Collector 1964
acrylic on canvas
60 × 72
Private collection

memory, using the idea of a seated Egyptian female figure and a contemporary-looking man drawn in a different style next to her. In a way, I was trying to combine two very different personalities. When I got back to London I did the paintings.

Not only is Hockney insouciant about combining disparate styles, but he feels the same way about including completely unrelated objects in the same rectangle. In 1964, he utilized the isometric framework of *The Second Marriage* in a work of entirely different character. *California Art Collector* is a serene conceit that takes place in indeterminate space. Now the top of the cube is the bright blue roof of a pavilion whose sides are defined by two thin, blue poles. Perched on a ponderous upholstered chair covered with a zany flower pattern is a stylized Hockney lady whose head merges with a monumental sculptured head suspended behind her. To complete the room are a few more anomalies; a second sculpture resembling a female figure and a spectacular rainbow that, for some reason, is "indoors" rather than over the pool.

During the late 1960s, Hockney's painting surface became increasingly refined as he lavished attention on rendering figures and objects in greater detail. Typical of this new approach was a succession of symmetrical double portraits of close friends, standing and seated in sparse interiors. For Hockney, these grand, neoclassic paintings were a new, if introspective, form of theater. In their austere settings, his characters are lost in their thoughts; they look inward, as it were, totally unconscious of their audience. Among the most impressive of these paintings is the 1969 double portrait of Henry Geldzahler and Christopher Scott. Geldzahler, then curator of contemporary art at the Metropolitan Museum, is ensconced, like a pasha, on a massive velour deco sofa in the middle of the canvas. To his right stands his friend Scott, whose form is symmetrically balanced at the left by a tall, torchère lamp. The rectangle of the window behind Geldzahler is echoed by the square glass coffee table in front of the couch. Commenting on this painting's relationship to a stage set, Hockney says:

It's interesting from the theatrical point of view because it uses absolutely one-point perspective. In fact, the vanishing point is actually just above Henry's head. I fastened strings to the painting to make the perspective work and all the lines converged over his head. It looked a bit like a halo with rays coming out, so I photographed it, because I was rather amused by it. It made Henry look angelic. He had just purchased that sofa and it was rather shabby. Later, he recovered it, but I "recovered" it first in the painting. The painting was made in London, although the room is in New York. I'd gone to New York for a week to make drawings, took a lot of photographs, and finally decided to rearrange the room. I rearranged things to give emphasis to the composition. It was painted the year after the double portrait of Christopher Isherwood and Don Bachardy, which also has a straightforward look. In that picture, a large

Henry Geldzahler and Christopher Scott 1969
acrylic on canvas
84 × 120
Abrams Family Collection

32

table in front of them comes up to the viewer. I don't think it's as theatrical as the one of Henry, because there the ground comes right up to you.

Geldzahler, with his distinguished fin-de-siècle appearance, is a frequent Hockney model, his well-trimmed beard and scholar's glasses contributing to his benign but authoritative appearance. Later, in the 1977 *Looking at Pictures on a Screen*, Hockney would again use him as his subject at the center of a painting. In that elegantly conceived work, an older, even more distinguished-looking Geldzahler calmly studies reproductions of masterpieces from London's National Gallery.

After this cool series of hieratically posed figured compositions, we see how Hockney combined his new academicism and the isometric box composition in the 1977 *Self-Portrait with Blue Guitar*. Now, the box, instead of defining the picture's outside contours, becomes a central element in it: now it is a massive table, at which the artist portrays himself seated, at work on a drawing. In this endless room, a Picasso-like sculpture of a head levitates against the outline of a window. The juxtaposition in this work of the lush blue curtain at the painting's right edge and the few diagonal lines that might or might not refer to walls and floors, seems perfectly logical. Though Hockney has a bewildering habit of combining massive and ephemeral forms in a single painting, the results are less jarring than lyrically surreal.

Situations in which real and illusionistic forms exchange identity appeal to Hockney. He admires the brilliant use of this principle in Jasper Johns's sculptures of everyday objects, such as light bulbs and Savarin coffee cans, which were cast in metal, then painted illusionistically to resemble their original selves. As his painting reveals, Hockney often favors the use of such artifice. The large canvas, *Model with Unfinished Self-Portrait*, was done while he was working on *Self-Portrait with Blue Guitar*. In the second picture the self-portrait has been placed in the background. In the foreground is the carefully rendered sleeping figure of Hockney's friend, Gregory Evans, wearing a blue robe. Hockney, in this multi-leveled composition, is psychologically as well as physically distant, while the sleeping Evans is more "real." Hockney explains the genesis of this static drama.

My self-portrait, which was not finished at the time, was leaning against the wall of my London studio. Gregory posed on a bed in front of it and a great deal of his figure was painted from life. That gave it a kind of power. It looks as though it's a painting of two completely different kinds of space. It seems as if there's a stage behind Gregory with a curtain. The curtain has been pulled back and there I am, about to draw a guitar.

Hockney's familiarity with the range of 20th-century art is attested to in numerous examples of his work that incorporate its celebrated themes and techniques.

An inveterate museum-goer, he frequently photographs works of art of all periods as he walks through galleries. Some of these gleanings, in considerably transmuted fashion, have been absorbed into his painting and theater imagery.

Looking at Pictures on a Screen 1977
oil on canvas
74 × 74
Collection Mr. and Mrs. Miles Q. Fiterman

In designing an opera production, the paramount task, Hockney asserts, is to interpret the composer's ideas—to find an equivalent in form and color for the music. Often he will use historical or modern styles as points of departure. Hogarth's 18th-century engravings for *A Rake's Progress* were the inspiration for Hockney's version. Fourteenth-century Italian panel painting and Old Kingdom Egypt are recalled in his *Magic Flute*. The masks used during the Stravinsky evening have their origins in Eskimo and Northwest Coast Indian art, Chinese painting and the Greek theater of Sophocles. While he is interested in the entire history of art, his major focus has been on early 20th-century art. The mannerisms of modernism—particularly French modernism—are echoed throughout his recent painting and theater projects. In his designs for the Metropolitan Opera's production of *Parade*, the immediate source was the voluptuous color and form of early 20th-century School of Paris painting.

To his discomfort, Hockney has occasionally found himself caught up in the irresolvable argument of figurative versus abstract art. While respectful of the accomplishments of the great nonobjective masters—particularly Mondrian and more recently Rothko—his wholehearted admiration is reserved for Picasso who probed the limits of realism and abstraction, then utilized these polarities to create dazzling new forms. Picasso's ability to turn space inside out and invest all subjects with humanistic content enthralls him. He is constantly impressed by his virtuosity as painter, draftsman, sculptor and creator of theater sets and, as he observes, however contradictory Picasso's stylistic explorations may seem—for example, Cubism versus Classicism—there can be no doubt that a single voice is speaking.

Hockney's utilization of art history has made him into something of a grand eclectic, a characterization he would not necessarily dispute. But as he points out, even his hero, Picasso, was not above lifting an idea or two if it would prove useful.

All artists are cannibals. With Picasso, though, it's very obvious because he took from so many sources. He used African and classical art. He copied Le Nain, he copied a lot of sooty academic painters, too. But it's like that with all artists. What do you think Van Gogh's copies of Millet look like? They certainly look like Van Gogh paintings that just happen to be copies of Millet. You have to work your way through a lot and take what you want.

And as to Picasso's working in a number of styles,

All you have to do is look at a number of Picasso's different periods to realize that whatever he did, his work is distinctive. We're so used to the way his hand moved and how he made the marks. No matter how many different directions he worked in, everything he did fits together and, because he produced such a volume of work, you can sense this consistency.

When, in 1980, the Walker Art Center presented an exhibition of works destined for the new Musée Picasso in Paris, Hockney came to Minneapolis to study it, explaining he was about to embark on a major design project for the

Model with Unfinished Self-Portrait 1977
oil on canvas
60 × 60
Collection Werner Boeninger

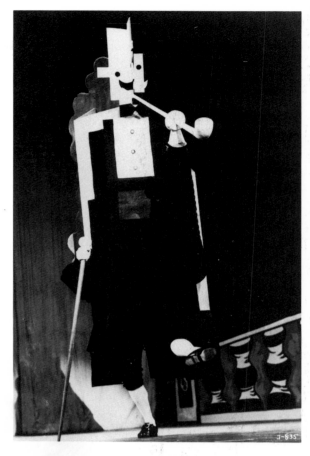

Philip Jerry as The Manager in Evening Dress in the Joffrey Ballet's 1973 production of Satie's *Parade*. The costumes were reproductions of those designed by Pablo Picasso for the 1917 Ballets Russes premiere of the Satie ballet.

(opposite)
Parade Stage Manager   1980
gouache on cardboard
16½ × 11¼

(p 40)
Iowa   1964
acrylic on canvas
60 × 60
Collection Hirshhorn Museum
and Sculpture Garden,
Smithsonian Institution

(p 41)
Portrait Surrounded by Artistic Devices   1965
acrylic on canvas
60 × 72
Collection Arts Council of Great Britain

Metropolitan Opera—the sets and costumes for *Parade*. Later that year, when The Museum of Modern Art held its monumental Picasso retrospective, Hockney was a frequent visitor. On view were reconstructions of several costumes designed by Picasso for the first production of *Parade* in 1917. These were fabricated for the Joffrey Ballet's 1973 revival of *Parade*. Wisely, Hockney decided that his version for the Metropolitan Opera would make respectful reference to that original conception and, indeed, he quoted several Picasso motifs in his costume designs, including the cubistic "stage manager" and the Chinese conjuror.

Hockney's admiration for Picasso's achievements, however, was evident well before his Met commission. His drawings and paintings of the 1960s contained frequent cubistic allusions; in addition to the 1964 *Cubist Boy with Colourful Tree*, other works echoed Cubism's various phases. In the elemental landscape, *Iowa*, 1964, the tree, barn, silo and clouds are reduced to bulky, geometric shapes. The 1965 *Portrait Surrounded by Artistic Devices*, with its seated man behind a pyramid of abstract cylinders, is a more sophisticated use of that style. Such standard cubist principles as simplified and flattened forms, tipped-up table and floor surfaces and shallow picture boxes, are now standard devices in Hockney's painting. Yet he is more than a facile borrower of styles, because he applies their formal principles in new ways. He is particularly interested in Cubism, the esoteric creation of Picasso and Braque, both for its space-altering properties and for its abstract syntax.

In his recent photographs more than in his paintings he has pursued his obsession with cubist space. Composed of numerous prints laid out mosaic fashion on white surfaces, these composite impressions vary from intimate interiors, to swimming pool pictures, to panoramas of the Grand Canyon and Yosemite—each subject recorded in his prismatic realism. The results, at once factual and highly inventive, indicate the way he perceives form.

I've often thought about the way I see. For years, I've thought my eyes are funny or something. I kept thinking how much can you really see and what is it you really take in as your eye moves about focusing? As your eye moves in space, it tells you about it. The space between you and what you see is very important. In my new photographs I deal with all the ground from under my feet on into deep space. My theory is, you must be aware of that. We are always conscious of the ground under us. Otherwise, no one would put a step forward. An ordinary photograph is like looking through a window. It's like traditional painting. The window implies a wall between you and what you see. In painting, the window was smashed eighty years ago by Cubism. In a recent issue of Aperture, *they quote me as saying there is no cubist photography. Yet, when you turn the page, there's an article on American cubist photographers.*

Mind you, if that's cubist photography, I'm Leonardo da Vinci. What they call cubist photography has only the most superficial aspects of Cubism. Those photographers didn't really come to grips with Cubism's ideas about space.

39

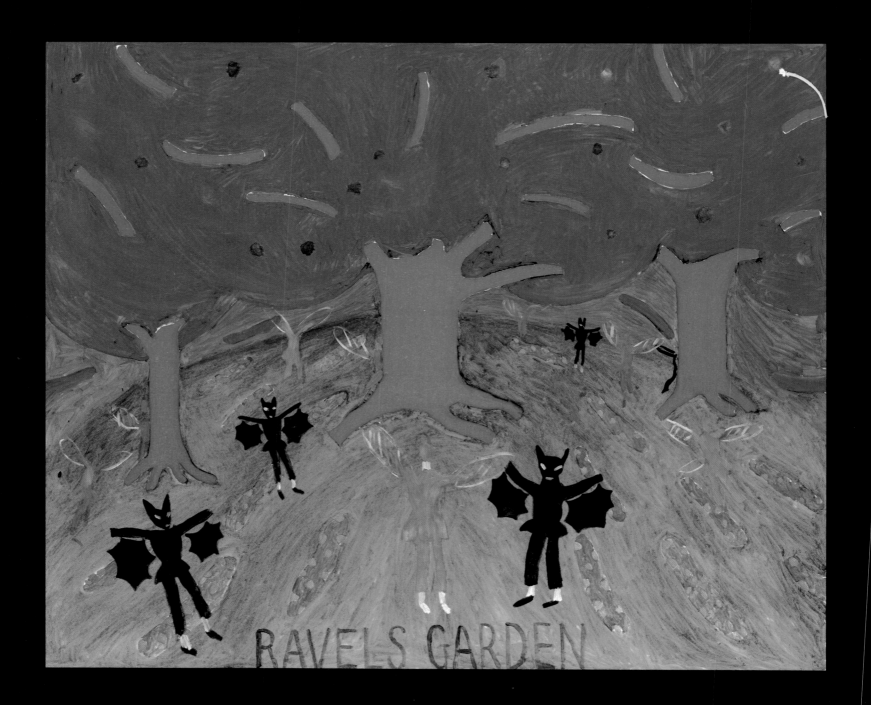

Cubism is all about space. Space is a thing in itself—an idea—not just something you see into.

Since the late 1970s, Hockney's major stylistic directions reflect the influences of early 20th-century French painting. While endlessly fascinated by Picasso, his interest in French art is not limited to that protean force. The tubular forms, for example, that compose the figures, still-life objects and landscape figures in Hockney's painting instantly recall Léger's pragmatic "mechanical" Cubism, that reduces everything to elegant, polychrome plumbing. A Miróesque ingenuousness flickers through his art and is especially apparent in his characterizations of the animals and insects in the Ravel opera. A distinctive south-of-France flavor, evocative of Matisse and Dufy, prevails even in his California paintings. His fluent line, spontaneously applied paint and lush washes relate it to that sunny tradition. Indeed, this French quality has actually intensified since he settled in California; it seems the nearby Pacific brings out the Mediterranean in him. Such full chroma reached an apogee in his brilliantly-hued sets for the Met's *Parade*. There was no question about *Parade*'s French ambience. The large, free-form blue, red and green shapes in *L'Enfant*'s garden scene are as evocative of Matisse as of childhood perceptions. Like the Fauve painters, Hockney allowed himself to regard the world with innocent eyes. The final image of the garden scene is an enormous tree whose thick red trunk and branches are abstract shapes that vibrate against dense blue foliage. Because he "sees" music coloristically, he sought to match Ravel's tonalities in color in his opera design. It is as if the child-hero of *L'Enfant* had envisaged the garden.

But how does Hockney feel about the stylistic changes his work undergoes as he moves from one opera production to another? The precise, detailed decor of *The Rake*, for example, contrasts sharply with *Parade*'s slapdash forms. On the surface, both productions would seem to reflect opposing artistic philosophies—but no, he says, each is a valid expression of his attitudes. Though the music and themes of successive opera projects have led him to new formal solutions, his basic ideas about form, space and color remain constant.

Nevertheless, he admits to a degree of restlessness and inability to stick with any particular style for long.

My work always jumps about. It's always moving in many directions and I believe that for twenty years there's never been a moment when it wasn't. There's always something left over from another painting—a few clues. I tend to push into little areas I've not explored; I also tend to drop something I've used for a long time and move on. I hate the idea of completely repeating myself. I understand how some artists can find a small area and pursue it extensively, and the best of them become subtle explorers of small things. Morandi did this with still life and Jasper Johns does it with many things and a varied art comes out of it. But I'm not that kind of person, nor does my mind work that way.

Ravel's Garden with Night Glow 1980
oil on canvas
60 × 72
Collection Mr. and Mrs. Morris S. Pynoos

Troop of Actors and Acrobats
drawing for *Parade* 1980
gouache, ink, pencil on paper
14 × 17

Chinese Conjuror
drawing for *Parade* 1980
gouache, pencil on paper
14 × 17

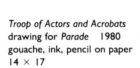

44

Hockney's ability to take what he needs from respected sources is admirably illustrated in his account of copying a Matisse painting.

I was staying at a house on Fire Island and a Matisse poster was on the wall. I had some wax crayons and thought I would make a copy of it while sitting at the table. When I pinned my copy to the wall, from a distance it looked like the Matisse—but it still contained my marks. At first, you couldn't see them very well, because the Matisse imagery dominated everything. I can't make marks like Matisse's. Everybody's hand moves in a different way.

While working on *Parade*, the relationship between Hockney's painting and stage design became extremely close and at times, these aspects of his creativity were inseparable. The sketches and gouaches made for *Parade* strongly affected his painting. That project was a liberating experience, as *Rake* had been earlier. As a consequence, his painting moved in freer directions, marked by large, expansive shapes, whose origins were in the brush stroke itself. Thanks to *Parade*, an energetic dialogue began between his studio and theater projects; one nourished the other.

To distinguish the exuberantly executed paintings that were by-products of *Parade* from Hockney's production designs can be daunting, because they share so many qualities of theme and style. *Parade*'s sets evolved from painted scale models he made for each scene. Many of his designs are fully-realized paintings. An example is the final study for *L'Enfant*'s garden scene, which Hockney submitted as a collage-painting to the Met's technical department. In this, the massive arboreal shape is a cutout, centrally placed over the verdant background.

To assist the costume shop in fabricating his *Parade* designs, Hockney made a series of small gouaches to describe the action in each scene and define each character's attire. Though loose and improvisational, these convey an astonishing amount of information. Arranged in chronological sequence, their effect is cinematic and the characters seem to move from one frame to another. The gouaches accurately foreshadowed what would occur on stage. By the time Hockney painted these, he knew every detail of *Parade*'s action as well as its decor. So certain was he about each scene, he could evoke it instantly on paper.

After completing designs for *Parade*, Hockney burned off some excess energy by painting some variations on a few modernist sources he had relied on. During the summer of 1980, in his London studio, he decided to reactivate his dialogue with recent art history. There, he rapidly produced a number of oils on music and dance themes. Some of these alluded to Picasso's *Parade*. The most recognizable was his interpretation of the ballet's celebrated curtain, with its bareback rider on a winged horse, matador and circle of seated harlequins. In his translation, Hockney enlarged the left side of the original curtain design. The winged horse remains, but now the bareback rider is visible only from the waist down—the upper half of her body is blocked by the top of the proscenium. Only two seated figures are left: a guitar

(p 46)
Parade Curtain after Picasso   1980
oil on canvas
48 × 60

(p 47)
Punchinello on and off Stage   1980
oil on canvas
48 × 36

strumming matador and a harlequin in a diamond-patterned leotard. Happily, Picasso's tri-colored, striped ladder has been retained. Hockney has used a "wet into wet" painting technique that enabled him to manipulate forms and develop complex, textured areas. In this and related paintings, he was less concerned with defining edges than creating rich surfaces from which forms would emerge organically.

Another in the Picasso-inspired series is *Punchinello on and off Stage*, a composition in which a dwarf punchinello in long, blond curls stands in the orchestra pit and faces the audience while a scene is played on stage. The drawing is deliberately chunky, with the innocence and forcefulness of a child's vision. In such works, we have further identification of Hockney's determination to rid himself, at least for the moment, of the refined descriptive line that for so long had been a hallmark of his work.

Of these summer 1980 paintings, the most fully-realized is *Harlequin*. Now, the enduring commedia dell'arte character appears in an environment of elemental forms, as much Hockney's as Picasso's: a patterned theater curtain that echoes the harlequin's costume, a pink pyramid and the French tri-color ladder. This composition became the Met's poster for the premiere of *Parade*. To accommodate its design to the opera house's vertical kiosks, Hockney provided the harlequin with a shelf of books on which to perform his handstand.

Even more generalized than the "modern art" outcroppings in his painting, is the southern California syndrome that now permeates his art. In his idealized reactions to its varied landscape we encounter smog-free aeries graced with tropical planting around azure swimming pools. Below the purple Hollywood Hills, the endless grid of Los Angeles extends into infinity.

His California subject matter ranges from the seedy to the opulent. Its deserted city squares fringed with spindly palms and its lively street theater have been frequent Hockney themes. The elegant patios and manicured lawns of Beverly Hills have become leitmotifs. However, as the symbol of his adopted home nothing equals the swimming pool. In his lyrical interpretations, light reflects off the water; solitary figures gaze into its depths; athletic youths are glimpsed beneath its shimmering surface.

His fascination with the pool theme is evident in a long sequence of paintings. In these languid vignettes, the pool becomes a luxurious form of open-air theater. In the 1964 *Picture of a Hollywood Swimming Pool*, Hockney uses skeins of broad blue lines to describe its surface. This style, in which a line twists, turns and creates syncopated, interlocking shapes, is reminiscent of Dubuffet's inspired scribbling in his *Hourloupe* paintings. The portrayal of water in *Sunbather*, 1966, by contrast, is as a flat pattern of tautly drawn spirals of confetti that fill the bottom three quarters of the canvas; at the top, the nude sunbather is modeled in Hockney's cool, classical realism. The figure-in-pool theme reaches something of an apotheosis in the 1966 *Portrait of Nick Wilder*. Now the water is an opulent mosaic of blue-green, cobalt and

Harlequin 1980
oil on canvas
48 × 36

(p 50)
Portrait of Nick Wilder 1966
acrylic on canvas
72 × 72
Private collection

(p 51)
Sunbather 1966
acrylic on canvas
72 × 72
Collection Museum Ludwig, Cologne

Harlequin.

sky blue areas. Wilder, then an art dealer in Los Angeles, is depicted in a near-photographic manner, his head and shoulders emerging from the tile-lined pool. In this serene, one-point perspective composition, the house functions as a painted backdrop whose windows, doors and long balcony are elements of a Mondrian-like grid.

In 1978, after Hockney had finished the *Magic Flute* sets, he spent several weeks at Tyler Graphics in Bedford Village, New York, where, using what for him was a new technique, he arrived at monumental abstract images whose origins were as much in the California pool paintings as in the geometry of the *Flute*. Though Ken Tyler's own swimming pool was the immediate subject for this cohesive group of images, their California ancestry is apparent. Tyler, a master printer who understands how to capture the interest of artists by presenting them with such irresistible blandishments as superb equipment and skilled technicians, came up with the notion of having Hockney do a number of works using handmade paper, another specialty of the studio. In this technique, paper pulp, a semi-liquid material permeated with color, is pressed into compartments defined by thin metal bands that follow the outline of the artist's design. Under the metal forms is placed a sheet of wet paper. Once the pulp has begun to harden and the major areas of the composition have been established, the artist can further work the surface by adding small increments of dyed paper pulp, using a ladle, a kitchen baster or some other instrument. The large, open shapes of the swimming pool theme were ideally suited to this process. Capitalizing on the possibilities of this malleable new medium, Hockney was able to capture the shimmering quality of water in successive variations. The heavily textured surfaces of the Paper Pools were to affect his approach to painting. Large color masses were allowed to establish their own perimeters.

With the Paper Pools, Hockney was able to build on two experiences: California and Egypt. His unquenchable attraction to the representation of water and admiration for the primal geometry of ancient Egyptian architecture are evident in this series. *Midnight Pool* (Paper Pool 10), 1978, is a large, six-panel image of a diving board cantilevered over an illuminated water surface. The massive shapes are strongly reminiscent of temple architecture in *The Flute*; the diving board suggests a monumental doorway. The pool's edges, in perspective, recall Glyndebourne's distinctive proscenium.

Though Hockney has lived in London, Paris and New York, he prefers Los Angeles. A hard-core devotee of the cinema since childhood, he had an idealized view of what might await him in Hollywood. This was a place blasé about social conventions, where eccentricity was barely noticed; life was easy and "laid-back." After the tensions and distractions of a brief stint in New York, he found California Edenesque. The privacy of a house, high in the hills, seemed the ultimate retreat. For one used to semi-nomadic existence, he took to house ownership with zeal—but, given his way of doing things,

Midnight Pool (Paper Pool 10) 1978
colored and pressed paper pulp
81½ × 92½
Collection Walker Art Center
Gift of Lindsay and Ken Tyler

53

matters did not simply end there. Inevitably, his house, like his friends, had to become a character in his visual dramas.

So taken was Hockney with the verdant jumble of the Hollywood Hills that in 1980 he made several paintings that reflect its vivid character. Among these free-wheeling evocations of the landscape are two large, rawly painted works, *Nichols Canyon* and *Mulholland Drive*. These are memory paintings, impressions of driving rapidly up, down and around the California hillsides with their twisting roads, clumps of vegetation, tile rooftops and an occasional electric pylon. The sights encountered while negotiating these roads vary from intimate views into stilt house interiors to spectacular vistas of downtown Los Angeles and the San Fernando Valley. There is little effort to accurately describe the complex terrain except as rhythmic monumental shapes reduced to flat patterns of violent color. In the gigantic *Mulholland Drive,* Hockney uses a whip line to define the contours of the local geography. Separate but interlocking areas, compartments of color—mainly blue-green, violet and orange tonalities—make up this dramatic painting. Each area is treated in a different manner; some are heavy with impasto, others are masses of pointillist color. *Nichols Canyon,* a vertical composition, is divided by a dark, curving roadway that symmetrically splits the painting. At close range the panorama is a constellation of buoyant, even strident color masses that have an abstract existence quite apart from the forms they describe.

Hockney has taken some great risks in these works. They have none of the refinement associated with the lyrical swimming pool paintings, but are violently expressionistic, revealing more concern with objectifying movement and feeling than describing details. They reveal the intuitive approach that underlay so much of the design for *Parade*, particularly the awesome garden scene in *L'Enfant.*

Off one of the many roads that form an erratic network above Sunset Boulevard, Hockney's house is virtually invisible from the street. Nestled into a hillside, the multi-storied wood and glass structure angles around an amoeba-shaped swimming pool whose sky-blue bottom is overlaid with a vibrant pattern of dark blue lines painted by Hockney to look like the ripples and waves in his pool pictures. Against the dense palm and giant ferns are brightly-colored canvas chairs.

The house began its existence as a middle-class Los Angeles hilltop dwelling of bland 1950s design. Its recent transformation has been an all-consuming project. "What do I need with a living room?" Hockney asks. "I don't live that way." Thus, the erstwhile living room, with the addition of a few skylights, has become a flexible work space, complete with drafting tables, large, metal print storage cabinets and stereo speakers obstructing traffic in the center. Around the fireplace are a few battered velour armchairs and a clunky wooden coffee table. Casually pinned to the white walls might be a few posters of recent Hockney exhibitions, some sketches and prints, or quantities of Polaroids made during a recent foray to the desert or during a visit to a

Nichols Canyon 1980
acrylic on canvas
84 × 60
Collection Mr. and Mrs. Richard C. Hedreen

55

Balcony, pool and steps, the artist's house
Hollywood 1982

Hollywood Hills House 1980
oil, charcoal, collage on canvas
60 × 120
Collection Walker Art Center
Gift of Mr. and Mrs. David M. Winton

friend's house. At the moment, he is adding a spacious, high-ceilinged studio in order to work on large-scale projects, paintings and set designs.

Beyond the utilitarian area, more colorful things are happening to the house. It has become a "work-in-progress." The exterior stucco is painted a muted pink; the balcony, extending the length of the house, and stairs to the pool are a strong ultramarine. The idea for investing the house with such personality came to Hockney while he was in London for Christmas in 1980. Depressed by the grim English winter, to cheer himself up he decided to make a painting of the California house from memory. The color of *Parade* was very much on his mind. The result was *Hollywood Hills House*, a large-scale triptych. In this highly subjective recollection, he allowed interior and exterior areas to flow into each other and the house appears as though in a dream. In contrast to his reasonably accurate portrayal of the living room, the outside is represented as a profusion of flat, abstract shapes laid out like a Matisse *papier collé*.

> *It shows everything I thought about the house. On the left panel you see the interior of the room with the fireplace and some things on the wall. On the floor are the set models for Ravel's garden and* Les Mamelles de Tirésias. *In the middle panel is the balcony, which then was natural redwood. In the painting it's red, not blue as it is today. There's a big palm tree in the middle of the picture. On the right you can see the curved brick wall around the pool and over it, yellow rays of sunshine. Making that painting gave me the idea to paint the house itself. At that time I was only renting it and the owners wanted to sell it, so either I had to move out or buy it. I was a bit fed up with moving around and had lived there two years, so I decided to buy it.*

> *Then, immediately, I had the outside painted. The colors were chosen from the Ravel opera. We used the bright green of the grass in the garden scene— that's what we did first. People thought I was a bit mad. My milkman from London—he delivers milk in Edwards Square—came to visit and painted the bricks on the windwall around the pool. Then I painted the swimming pool. Every two or three months we would make a few color changes. Then, because of what we were doing, I began making more paintings of the outside of the house.*

> *Recently we started having the inside of the house painted, using brighter colors. I started by carrying the pink from the outside into the house. I realized you could bring the outside in because now you were looking through windows at color all the time. It was partly seeing the De Stijl exhibition at the Walker that inspired me to paint the inside. I looked through the catalogue—lots of strong color—the red, blue, gray, yellow. Then I also remembered that Monet painted the inside of his Giverny house yellow. I remembered going there and suddenly realized that, in a sense, I was doing the same thing. He made his house and garden an environment that he used as subject matter for many years. I can understand a painter doing that.*

The *Hollywood Hills House* picture and the subsequent transformation of the

house itself made clear that the old process was reversed; now, Hockney's theater design was influencing the course and content of his painting.

Today, the hilltop house is in chronic mild chaos. The evidence of various projects—paintings, photographs and theater models—is scattered about. The phone rings constantly with requests for loans of paintings for exhibitions, invitations to lecture and to dinner, as well as calls from friends from near and far who just want to chat. There are numerous visitors—fellow artists, collectors, relatives and friends of relatives from Bradford. On any given day, the housekeeper picks her way through piles of clothing, books and papers; the housepainter makes it impossible to negotiate the narrow hallway.

Above the smog line, the house was meant to be Hockney's bastion against the pressures and blandishments of the outside world. This, however, has never been the case, given his penchant for taking on new projects. He is in England several times a year working on projects at his Pembroke Gardens studio or visiting his family in Bradford. Frequent exhibitions of his paintings and photographs in New York and abroad, printmaking projects at Ken Tyler's studio, a conference on handmade paper in Japan, lectures at museums and universities, keep him on the move.

He works constantly, sketching objects and people around him during conversations or pointing his Pentax camera around the room. He has remarkable ability to focus on a point, no matter what the distractions, recalling in precise detail the circumstances of making a particular painting. Soft-spoken and unfailingly polite, he expresses himself eloquently on a variety of art and non-art issues. He has the Yorkshireman's ability to characterize a situation with incisive wit and is a superb raconteur. He has clearly come to terms with himself as an individual and an artist. Though now an establishment figure, he is set apart by his attire. His approach to clothing continues to be haphazard and inventive. His costume can vary from ployglot color and pattern one day to almost conventional apparel on another.

At his best, Hockney is a walking collage. While working at the Metropolitan Opera he would occasionally turn up in a red and white baseball cap, paint-spattered, high-waisted, 1940s-style pin-stripe trousers held up with red suspenders, a rumpled white shirt with a neon blue and yellow striped tie, and a pair of arresting multi-colored, wing-tipped oxfords. Recently he gave up his familiar black-rimmed round glasses in favor of a more elegant pair consisting of a metal circle for one eye and a tortoise one for another. In light of his daily dress, it's no wonder he has been able to come up with such inventive costume ideas for his operas. On a good day he would be completely at home in *Parade*'s opening crowd scene.

So closely related are Hockney's views about theater design and painting that his sustained involvement with Glyndebourne and the Metropolitan can hardly be regarded as peripheral activities. Opera's improbable themes have provided him with new subject matter, rich in formal possibilities. In the same way that, as a young artist, he had turned to literary sources, he now mines opera's sumptuous repertory.

Interior, Pembroke Studios,
London, 1982

The Rake's Progress

a fable

libretto by W.H. Auden and Chester Kallman

decor by David Hockney
assisted by Mo McDermott

after W. Hogarth

music by Igor Stravinsky

Produced by John Cox

Text to Image

Stephen Spender

The idea of a painter who previously has designed but one work for the stage (in Hockney's case *Ubu Roi*) being brought into the opera house to design sets and costumes has about it something suspect. I think that many people, on hearing in the 1970s that Hockney was designing sets for the opera festival at Glyndebourne, must have envisaged works that would be done in the familiar manner of his paintings and drawings. But, although his stage pictures were seen to be very recognizably Hockney, people who attended the first night in Glyndebourne of *The Rake's Progress* in 1975 or of *The Magic Flute* in 1978, both designed by him, soon realized that what they were witnessing was not Stravinsky or Mozart tailored to Hockney's idiosyncratic art, but the composer's music transformed into the artist's vision which had somehow achieved the miracle of completely absorbing the music. Here was a true marriage of the arts.

The fundamental reason for the extraordinary success of Hockney's designs for the opera is that his passion for music is at least as great as his passion for painting. An intense and close observer, whose most constant facial expression is that of his eyes being screwed up with looking, he listens with as great intensity as he looks. He is an addict of the Sony Walkman and, with earphones over his head, walks along the pavement or drives his car or lies upon the floor of his house, listening perhaps to *The Barber of Seville* or perhaps *The Magic Flute* or perhaps to *Oedipus Rex* or perhaps to the music he most cherishes—Ravel's *L'Enfant*. The Sony Walkman takes Hockney away from his surroundings. "I can walk along the street or in a public garden and be completely cut off from all the other people there, in a world of total happiness and enjoyment, all my own," he once said to me—a remark which sometimes makes me nervous when driving with him, if, at the same time, he is listening to a performance of, say, *The Barber of Seville*, as he once was when rushing past Notting Hill Gate.

Hockney has common sense, is a sharp social commentator, is, in fact, in

Drop Curtain for The Rake's Progress 1975–79
ink on paper and cardboard
13⅞ × 20⅛

The great wall of fire from Act II of *The Magic Flute*, as performed at Glyndebourne Festival Opera, 1978

many ways a representative member of a generation for whom Elvis Presley and the Beatles were heroes. With so much about him of shared taste, it is important to emphasize that despite his receptiveness to the pleasures and fashions surrounding him, he inhabits a world of things seen and heard which is uniquely his own. The meeting of his musical with his pictorial preoccupations brings out the originality he makes of his eclecticism. In the settings—especially in the effects of color and light—as in the second act of *The Magic Flute*, he becomes a visionary artist. His vision is the music.

In *The Magic Flute* the three tiers of characters—Tamino and Pamina, Papageno and Papagena, Sarastro and Priests—with their separate but related stories scarcely ever converging, have musical idioms suited to each, developing parallel throughout the opera. On each of these levels Hockney translates the music into his visual symbolism, drawn from the almost surrealist engravings of Egyptian sculpture and monuments of Piranesi and from Italian primitive painting: the bird forms of Papageno and Papagena; the trials through fire and water of the music; the architectonic splendor of the mystical religious music; the progression of the opera from the stylized opening scene in the temple gardens, through the architecture of the temple, to the near abstract effects of pure color and light of the later mystical religious scenes.

Hockney knows a lot about painting, a lot about music, and quite a lot else though he has the appearance of the self-educated. One is, in fact, always a bit surprised at how much he knows, for example how much poetry he has read and can recite. For he does not strike one as being a learned artist—in the way, say, that Eliot and Auden were learned and looked it. Under his considerable sophistication, he remains fundamentally naive, childlike even—a fact of which he is aware in a way that shows loyalty to childhood. So what surprised critics of his designs for operas was the extent to which he had acquired background information about each work and showed historic sense. The Metropolitan triple bill of *Parade*, *Les Mamelles de Tirésias* and *L'Enfant et les Sortilèges* brought the aesthetic excitement associated with the legendary names of Picasso, Apollinaire, Satie, Ravel and Poulenc into the New York of the 1980s. The sets for *The Rake's Progress* are faithful to Hogarth, in whose famous series of paintings and engravings Stravinsky found inspiration. "Everything in it comes from Hogarth," Hockney told me.

To the surprise of many critics Hockney, in his designs for *The Magic Flute*, paid great attention to the stage directions and records of the original Vienna production at the Theater auf der Wieden in 1791, a source despised, disdained and passed over by most producers of the opera, who regard Schikaneder, the original impresario, director, librettist, player of the role of Papageno and friend of Mozart, as little better than a mountebank, who made the plot almost incomprehensible in attempting to tailor it to suit the Viennese public.

The lively and irreverent Hockney, always conscious of his working class origins in Bradford, Yorkshire, reading about *The Magic Flute* must, I think,

William Hogarth
Hudibras Beats Sidrophel, Plate VIII
from Samuel Butler's *Hudibras*   1725–26
engraving
9¹¹/₁₆ × 13⅝

William Hogarth
A Rake's Progress, Plate VIII   1735
engraving
12⅜ × 15¼
Collection The Art Institute of Chicago

have felt sympathy for Schikaneder who worked his way up from poverty to become director of the Theater auf der Wieden, where he put on performances of *Singspiele* (popular musical comedies). Hockney is certainly Mozartian in liking the idea that the basis or base of the pyramid (like those pyramids which are symbolic forms in the Masonic cult) of art should be its popularity—the apex sublime, and striking the stars. He sees *The Magic Flute* as a fairy story, like Shakespeare's *The Winter's Tale*. Fairy story, fable, parable, ascend by way of yokels, country bumpkins and coarse lovers—Autolycus in Shakespeare, Papageno and Papagena in Mozart—to the romantic lovers who have to endure trials and tests which sanctify their union, until the apex of the pyramid is reached in the music of the Masonic cult (reaching to what is sacred in all mystical religion) of which Sarastro is High Priest.

Hockney's approach to stage designing is a process of saturation. Saturation first in the music, then in the libretto, then in the history of the work and its past productions. He told me that he loved the libretto of *The Rake's Progress* before he came to love the music which was not entirely sympathetic to him. It was only after he had listened to *The Rake* a great many times that he came to love it. Love is the operative word. Love for the language of Auden and Kallman leading to love for the music, and love for the paintings and engravings of Hogarth's *A Rake's Progress* are the preconditions of his designs.

Richard Wagner put forward the idea of a fusion of the arts of music and drama—singing, acting and scenic design—but, in *The Ring*, it is only the oceanic combination of voice and orchestra in unending melody and recurrent leitmotifs which achieve a fusion. In fact, Wagner's scenery remained a kind of cave for singers, and his stage properties—anvils, swords—were labels stuck onto his leitmotifs. Music-drama was really achieved—though mostly without voices—by Diaghilev's Ballets Russes in which the solo dancers become symbols of the surrounding music, scenery and developing story line, the musculature of their bodies as submissive to this as the poetic symbols within a poem by Mallarmé. In the Diaghilev ballet the dancer becomes the object of the music and the action.

Hockney, whose first stage designs were for the 1896 surrealistic satire *Ubu Roi* of Alfred Jarry, surely began by absorbing his ideas of a fusion of the arts on the stage from the Ballets Russes and Picasso. The music drama of Satie and Poulenc, Apollinaire and Ravel, grew out of the interrelationships of a group of poets, painters and composers, not just of theories thought up by them. This was true Left Bank Paris, a village of the arts. The idea of going back to this period was in part what appealed to Hockney, when in his production of the three one-act works at the Met, he wreathed barbed wire round the stage in each work, to suggest the link with wartime Paris, 1917. In the Metropolitan production he designed scenery and sets with witty references throughout to Picasso, Braque, Dufy and other French artists, stage pictures transformed into unique Hockney. No one demonstrates more clearly than Hockney in his work for the stage, that an artist can owe

David Hockney and Celia Birtwell picnic at the opening of *The Rake's Progress*, Glyndebourne Festival Opera, 1975

and acknowledge that he owes a great deal to the past and yet be completely original.

At Glyndebourne Hockney was doubtless influenced by the fact that he was designing sets and costumes for an ideal small opera house, situated in the opulent, green Sussex countryside, the realized dream of an eccentric millionaire (now dead), John Christie. There is an atmosphere at Glyndebourne of aristocratic grandeur and noblesse. Christie wished that, during the evenings of high summer of the Glyndebourne festival, all members of the audience should wear evening dress. Some booked their places at the restaurant, and during the main interval were served excellent food and chateau-bottled vintage wine. Others strolled through exemplary gardens or picnicked on spacious lawns. If the standards of performance had not been supremely high, and if music lovers had not been prepared to pay sacrificial sums for their Glyndebourne evenings, all this would have been ludicrously anachronistic. But there is something authoritatively nostalgic about Glyndebourne as though the past has established a just claim to criticize the present.

On the first evening of the first performance of *The Magic Flute* to which my wife and I went, there was an outdoor party on the lawns after the performance, with food and drink served from long tables. There was something greenly, sumptuously, exceptionally English about seeing guests, performers, David Hockney and the director, John Cox, enjoying their triumph on that occasion, a fête champêtre at which one might have found Mozart and Stravinsky toasting one another and the artist and performers. Such Englishness can be unforgettable and I need scarcely apologize if there seems something snobbish about it. Glyndebourne creates its atmosphere which is to be a setting for productions which are jewels and I think awareness of the splendid occasion shows in David Hockney's designs for *The Magic Flute*.

I asked Hockney how he approached the problem of doing these set designs and costumes. He replied that after listening a great deal to the music and studying Schikaneder's directions, what struck him above all else in the opera was the combination of the comically human (which must on no account be lost sight of) with the awesomely religious in what he called the "unbelievably clear" music. Schikaneder tried to make his libretto and production competitive with other Viennese *Singspiel*. Obviously the idea of Egypt in Vienna in 1791 did not suit the Glyndebourne audience of 1978. So Hockney, who had recently gone as a tourist to Egypt, asked himself what kind of Egypt would work today. Only an Egypt which incorporated a past Biblical vision of ancient Palestine would appeal to the modern audience.

He considered first of all a kind of stylized realism rather in the manner of Piranesi's engravings, but rejected this. Yet I think that something of Piranesi does get into some of the stage-pictures. For example, in the scenes of the Temple, there are three pillared temples surmounted by pediments. Inscribed above the portal of one is VERNUNFT (reason), on the second WEISHEIT

Giovanni Battista Piranesi
Ancient Baths (F126)
from *Opere varie di architettura* 1750
etching
5½ × 7¾

(p 66)
A Rocky Landscape
model for *The Magic Flute* 1977
photographs on cardboard, paint on
molded cardboard, tissue, wire
16 × 21 × 12¼

Water
model for *The Magic Flute* 1977
photographs on cardboard, wire, tissue
16¼ × 21¼ × 12

(p 67)
Fire
model for *The Magic Flute* 1977
photographs on cardboard, wire, tissue
16 × 21¼ × 12

(wisdom), and on the third NATUR (nature). These have the character not of Piranesi's topical engravings, but of his studies of architecture, examples of which Hockney must have often seen at the London apartment of his friends Nikos Stangos and David Plante.

The opening scene of Hockney's *Magic Flute* has the character of early Renaissance Italian painting of rocky deserts and of chiseled, sculptured, grooved and hollowed out mountains seen beyond a tawny-colored foreground of sand. A few scattered trees are painted in leafy detail with loving observation, a bit comic looking and with something of trees in Los Angeles. This desert is ascetic, pure but not a terrifying solitude. For it is, like the deserts of Italian trecento painters, totally in the control of the artist, the warmth of his loving, creative hand pressing everywhere. In some miraculous way, although so candidly indebted to the past, it is in no way pastiche, but entirely Hockney, with touches of his humor. This confrontation of humor with ascetic religious feeling—the clarity of music made visible to the eye—becomes explicit with the entry of the dragon in pursuit of Tamino. The contradictions of comic pantomime with supreme religious hymn and with human love (reaching with Pamina to poignant heights—coarse and jovial with Papageno and Papagena—rapacious with the Moor) seem projected from Mozart's music into Hockney's designs. This results firstly from Hockney's complete absorption in the music, and after that, from his cheerful acceptance of all the inconsistencies of action and plot, and his ability to reconcile these differences in his designs as Mozart does in the music.

Hockney sees *The Magic Flute* as a journey—a progression, central to which is the search for each other and the coming together, after frustration and trials, of the two lovers, Tamino and Pamina. There is a parallel progression of religious seeking in the work, realized in the sacred music. So long as these progressions are maintained, the notorious contradictions—the star-flaming Queen of the Night becoming a dark villainess, Sarastro, the tyrant, becoming a high priest of righteousness—do not greatly matter. The love of Papageno and Papagena falls into place, paralleling and partly parodying that of Tamino and Pamina like the coarse working-class lovers in a Dickens novel, underscoring the repressed and sublimated loves of the upper-class characters. Hockney brings out in his interpretation of *The Magic Flute* the Renaissance theme of sacred and profane love: Tamino and Pamina sacred, Papageno and Papagena profane.

In the second act Hockney used many scene changes—thirteen in all, I think he said—to emphasize the theme of a journey. The whole opera moves from darkness into light, all of the action taking place in darkness except at the end, when the sun comes out. A difficulty, Hockney explained to me, was to paint darkness. The only way of doing so was to use rich earth colors.

All the indoor action of *The Magic Flute* takes place in a temple, the outdoor scenes being in a garden on the temple grounds. These include a mountain in which there is the scene of the trials by fire and water through

which Tamino and Pamina pass. Hockney renders this with the visionary, terrifying intensity of an early English romantic painter, Blake or Palmer. The fleece-like waters curl down over steps, the flames rise upwards in stalagmites to meet clouds that descend on them like stalactites.

As the music and action proceed to the interior of the temple, the sets become more geometrical (like Piranesi's illustrations of architectural forms) and even abstract. The music becomes increasingly pure and sacred and the stage pictures correspondingly so. This is not abstract art, it is pure music rendered by art purged of all distraction from the music. Hockney remarked that against this exaltation of the religious theme there runs across the stage the pantomime action of Papageno and Papagena. "We're laughing at Papageno, but we have to believe in him," he said. Against eternal skies Papagena provides the comedy of our lives.

The Magic Flute stage pictures achieve marvelous unity out of diversity. *The Rake's Progress* has the unity of a single, consistent, deliberately artificial style.

Hockney's approach to Stravinsky is as different as possible from his approach to Mozart, the difference arising from the fact that *The Magic Flute* is in a very important sense romantic, whereas *The Rake's Progress*, in the interpretation of Hogarth's sequence of pictures of the decline and fall of an 18th-century rake by the librettists, W. H. Auden and Chester Kallman, and in Stravinsky's music, is neoclassical modernism. By romanticism in *The Magic Flute* I mean that the members of the audience can identify with the lovers in Mozart's music and in Hockney's sets. The classicism of *The Rake's Progress* lies in the ironic detachment of composer and librettists—carried out onto the visual plane by Hockney—from the characters and story. composer and librettists seem to stand outside the tragedy of Tom Rakewell's decline and fall, while the audience regards the events that take place on the stage as pure spectacle which scarcely involves them emotionally, though the music itself— and for that matter the scenery—may move them by its beauty, occasional feeling and depths of truth. The audience does not identify with the loves of Anne Trulove and Tom Rakewell. It is a kind of mechanism like a Swiss cuckoo clock. The music of Anne has pathos without the character herself feeling pathetic.

The Rake is of course a parable of human folly, wickedness and suffering but one seems to regard it from a great distance, the 18th century seen through the wrong end of a 20th-century telescope. The music, while in a modern idiom, is also a pastiche of an old one, and the same thing is true of Hockney's sets which, while as modern as Hockney himself, are also pastiches of Hogarth. We are never allowed to forget, listening and looking, that what we hear and see on the stage is based a sequence of pictures depicting a moral story enacted in the 18th century.

Stravinsky and Hockney have it in common that they can both make a completely modern work most recognizably their own out of the elements

UNLIKE VERDI

Baba the Turk
sketch for *The Rake's Progress*   1975
collage, ink on paper
14 × 11

of some past work which arouses their admiration, a characteristic shared by the librettists, Auden and Kallman, whose language here is based on 18th-century pastorals and vers de société. Hockney deliberately multiplies those effects of distancing and objectifying that are present in the music and libretto. He reads the text, conscious of its complexities. He invents the image of the Bread Machine corresponding to the considerable intellectual complexity of Auden and Kallman's preoccupation with the *acte gratuité* demonstrated in Tom Rakewell's arbitrary decision, made at the suggestion of Shadow, to exercise his freedom of will by marrying—not according to the choice of his senses, but against it—Baba the Turk, who is repulsive to him. Shadow tells Tom Rakewell to act freely, to ignore those twin tyrants of appetite and conscience. He counsels him to take Baba the Turk to wife.

Hockney takes from Hogarth's series scenery, costumes and stage properties, innumerable details. In the background of the scene in the madhouse there is an explosion of Hogarthian detail drawn like graffiti on the imprisoning walls. He might so easily have simply transposed Hogarth's paintings into stage pictures but he has done something much subtler than that. In order to distance the action from stagey realism, he has taken a hint from the engravers of the Hogarth series of paintings and made stage pictures with the engravers' line, hatching and crosshatching both scenery and costumes. The entire opera is visualized as engravings, making pictures that look two-dimensional, thus emphasizing their artifice. Color is introduced to give the effect of prints painted over in watercolors. The effect of distancing, objectifying, is underlined by making the stage sets and costumes look like ironical pastiches of Hogarth's already ironical satire.

On the stage, rooms look like boxes in which characters are trapped, the only exception being a backcloth painted to look like an engraving in the opening scene of Tom Rakewell setting forth from the Trulove household on his journey. In the madhouse scene, boxes proliferate into docks which look like prison cells; in each is a madman or madwoman. Perhaps, designing this scene, Hockney remembered lines from T. S. Eliot's *The Waste Land:* "We think of the key, each in his prison / Thinking of the key, each confirms a prison." The action conveys the progression—or regression—from the house of the respectable bourgeois Trulove and his daughter Anne, to whom Tom Rakewell is betrothed, through the scenes in Mother Goose's Brothel and Tom's London house, to Bedlam and churchyard, death and delirium. The opera ends with a moralistic epilogue declaimed by the character before the curtain, in the manner of the Epilogue to Mozart's *Don Giovanni*. Stravinsky, Auden, Kallman and Hockney are all extremely sophisticated in their awareness of precedents.

In *The Magic Flute* Hockney visualizes emotions of love, religion and the sensual living of ordinary human beings which has to be accepted. In *The Rake's Progress* he visualizes the 18th-century morality of Hogarth as seen through modern eyes and yet fixed in the distance of its past. In both works,

Bread Machine
sketch for *The Rake's Progress*   1975
ink on paper
14 × 17

70

Study for Bedlam
sketch for *The Rake's Progress*   1975
ink on paper
10 × 10

Sarastro
drawing for *The Magic Flute*   1978
crayon
14 × 17

as in his designs for *L'Enfant*, *Parade* and *Le Rossignol*, his deepest insights come from his being inspired by the music. It would be wrong to say that some of the sets for *L'Enfant*, *The Magic Flute* and *The Rake's Progress* excel his paintings. What is true is that he has invented here something different from the paintings, supreme of its kind. Like the animals in the scene in which Tamino is an Orpheus who tames wild beasts with the sounds of the magic flute, he has submitted his genius to the music, transforming the characteristics of a visual artist into musical color, line and symbolism. *The Magic Flute* is a medley, a great many things finally woven into a commedia dell'arte: the farce of animal humanity (Pagageno); the tests of human love (Tamino and Pamina); sacred love (Sarastro)—and a good deal more variety. Take away the words and you have something like a symphony in which allegro, andante and scherzo all go on at different levels. It is a parable of the multiplicity of human life.

Considered purely as plot and characterization, the libretto is notoriously self-contradictory. The transformation of the Queen of the Night—first appearing as her daughter Pamina's semi-divine protectress and guardian of her love for Tamino—into a malevolent witch and hatcher of wicked plots, is confusing as action and plot, but not, perhaps, in the music. Nor is it perhaps contradictory on that level of the imagination, where in a fairy story a beautiful queen might well be transformed into a wicked stepmother and witch. It does not really matter that Sarastro, cast for the role of tyrant in Tamino's recitative, *ein Unmensch, ein Tyrann* (a monster, a tyrant) turns out to be the holy priest of a cult. To the modern audience such contradictions—guardian mother who is also wicked witch, inhuman tyrant who is also wise priest—are merely psychological complexities resolved anyway in the fact that in the mind of the mother, Sarastro is a wicked alienator of her daughter's affections, and in the mind of Sarastro (male chauvinist pig supreme) the Queen of the Night is woman diabolic. Nor does Mozart's freemasonry really present any obstacle to a modern audience which accepts in the poetry of W. B. Yeats his esoteric occult religious symbolism. If *The Magic Flute* were in accord with Mozart's Catholicism, it might seem to be church music and present a modern public with more difficulties than the mystery of music that expresses the sense of the sacred at all times.

In *The Magic Flute* the three strands of action—each with its musical idiom, comical, romantic and classically sacred—diverge and also intertwine. The opera retains its hold over us because this confluence of separate views of life—all of them true—permeated with mysterious forces like "the music of the spheres"—influencing our fates—is true to the complexity of life.

The libretto of *The Magic Flute* has its felicities—words which Mozart picks up and makes wonderful: the *sei standhaft, duldsam und verschwiegen* (be firm, patient and taciturn)—with little drum taps pointing up each word of the three boys; Tamino's aria, *Dies Bildnis ist bezaubernd schön* (This picture is bewitchingly beautiful) with its wonderful stretching out of the word *vielleicht* (maybe) in the music; and ecstatic *Sie ist's* (It is she) and *Er ist's* (It is he) of Tamino and Pamina, recognizing each other. In such places the words simply become the music. In such passages the music seems to invent the words, or, to put it differently, Mozart seems to pick on words and phrases which he can transfigure in the music, making of them a language beyond words.

In *The Rake's Progress* the Auden/Kallman libretto has an authority all its own that sometimes seems to stand outside the music. There are things which seem clearer in the words and in Hockney's visual symbolization of them, such as the Bread Machine, that scarcely have a musical equivalent. Stravinsky asked to be fed with Auden's words for which he felt a deep respect. Quite rightly, Hockney looked first at the libretto and then turned to the music which, eventually, he came to like as much as he did the words. With *The Magic Flute* he went first to the music and then to Schikaneder.

The subject of *The Rake's Progress*, based on Hogarth, is overtly a morality tale about the downfall of the reckless, extravagant Tom Rakewell, who willingly falls into evil hands, and the forgiving love for him of Anne Trulove. It is a tale in whose extravagant stage properties Hogarth luxuriates. It has nothing of the Salvation Army about it. And Auden/Kallman, Stravinsky and Hockney also luxuriate in it, Hockney managing to introduce into his sets every stage property and detail that exists in Hogarth. The morality part becomes a convention upon which the writer, composer and artist construct a common style of modern sophistication which contains deliberate elements of ironic pastiche based on Hogarth and, in Stravinsky's music, based on Mozart. There is also another modern morality play superimposed on the Hogarthian morality of the way of the world. The modern morality, advanced in the libretto, is existentialist and Christian: life is a game of sensation into which the central character, Rakewell, throws himself to taste it to the utmost. Tom is not really in search of pleasure. He seeks the sensations that give the utmost sense of being alive. These include despairing and loving. They make infidelity to any marriage engagement with Anne inevitable, because marriage blunts extremes of sensation. *Le mariage, c'est l'ennui* (Marriage is a bore), Jean Cocteau once said to me. And this is the modern view if you want, like Tom Rakewell, to taste the extremes of sensuality, riches, madness, death (as several recent poets, to take an obvious example, have done). Rakewell is really more like Arthur Rimbaud, Dylan Thomas or John Berryman than like Hogarth's hero, though there is obviously a connection between the 18th-century gambling dens and brothels and New York bars and existential "pads."

The Rake's Progress pushes the game beyond madness to the point where it becomes a game with death, and, beyond death, with God. This happens in libretto, score, and in Hockney's sets which progress from the flat backcloths with the singers standing in front of them of the first scenes, to the engulfing brothel room enclosing revelers and purchasers in the central scene, to the

74

imprisoning separation of each within his box-like stall of the mad scene and ending with the churchyard.

Every opera goer would agree, I suppose, that despite confusion of plot and character in his music, Mozart has woven the strands of action of *The Magic Flute* into a unity of style unique to it: entirely different from his other operas and from any other opera by any other composer. Hockney has discovered in his sets visual counterparts for the separate strands of plot and characters and, like Mozart, woven them into what might be called a visual-musical unity. His designs for *The Magic Flute* are as unique to that work as Mozart's music. If he goes on to do other stage sets one can be quite certain that they will be no more like this than are his designs for *Parade*, *Le Rossignol*, or *L'Enfant*. For *The Rake's Progress* he has also created a unique style, though it is wittily and beautifully related to the fact that Stravinsky's opera itself is based on the art of Hogarth. Hockney has, as it were, gone back to Hogarth, mixed it with Stravinsky, and with Auden and Kallman, and then produced something entirely Hockney, which is yet very closely related to all of theirs, indeed rooted in his loving experiencing of them. His uniqueness as a designer of operas is that he is able to absorb himself so completely in the music that he can translate it into visual images which are themselves musical, and yet which contain qualities of his idiosyncratic and recognizable vision.

Translations of the music.

Garden Scene from *The Rake's Progress*
as performed at Glyndebourne Festival Opera, 1975
Father Trulove: Don Garrard
Anne Trulove: Jill Gomez
Tom Rakewell: Leo Goeke
Nick Shadow: Donald Gramm

Auction Scene from *The Rake's Progress*
as performed at Glyndebourne Festival Opera, 1975
Sellem, an auctioneer: John Fryatt
Baba the Turk: Rosalind Elias
and members of the Glyndebourne Festival Opera Chorus

Baba the Turk

The Auctioneer

Baba
Wedding dress

from "The Rakes Progress, Glyndebourne June 1975

Hockney at Glyndebourne

John Cox and Martin Friedman

**"I suppose, if you're asking me,
you're wanting something a bit out of the ordinary!"**
(David Hockney to John Cox on being invited
to design *The Rake's Progress* for the Glyndebourne Festival Opera.)

When the Glyndebourne Festival Opera decided to produce *The Rake's Progress*, John Cox favored David Hockney as the ideal artist to design the sets. Earlier, there had been some discussion about having the *Sunday Times* political cartoonist, Gerald Scarfe, do the job, but Cox demurred. For him, Hockney's work projected a love of humanity, a quality the director deemed essential in telling the story of the once-innocent Tom Rakewell whose pact with the devil would lead to his ruin. In his own words, John Cox has been with the Glyndebourne Festival "on and off, man and boy, since 1959" and in 1971 became its director of production.

He was looking for an unconventional approach that would allude to the 18th-century Hogarthian origins of the Rake theme, yet emphatically modern in the spirit of its composer, Igor Stravinsky. As Hockney recalls, the invitation came at a particularly difficult time, when his drawing and painting had reached their most intense academicism and he was casting about for an escape from sheer technique. The Rake theme, which he had pursued in his barely post-art-student days, was especially enticing; in 1961–63 he had made a series of etchings on that subject and it was a simple matter to reimmerse himself in it. This new experience of working on an opera and responding to Stravinsky's exhilarating music and the brilliant Auden/Kallman libretto, resulted in one of the most inventive manifestations to occur on Glyndebourne's stage. So well received was the first Cox/Hockney collaboration that a year later they teamed up again for *The Magic Flute*. With this second successful joint venture, it was apparent that Hockney's

An Assembly
study for *The Rake's Progress*   1975
colored inks, cut and pasted paper on paper
19¾ × 25⅝
Collection The Museum of Modern Art, New York
Gift of R. L. B. Tobin

talents were not limited to the design of 20th-century opera and that he could, with originality and style, take on the classics.

As soon as they began working together, it was evident to Cox that Hockney was no conventional designer; he was cheerfully free with suggestions for all aspects of the production, not only for its visual character. For *The Rake's Progress* and *The Magic Flute* he prepared himself thoroughly, familiarizing himself with nuances of the music and libretto, and explored, through numerous sketches and cardboard models, ways of interpreting these. From the start, he thought of himself as a full partner in these enterprises, with definite views about the character of the evenings and as Cox recalls, the collaborative process was challenging and unpredictable.

The working arrangement between David Hockney and me was different from that normally operating between director and designer. A stage designer, like a director, at least insofar as drama and opera are concerned, is mere interpreter. With David, it was a case of inviting an artist established in his own right to come in and use the operas as inspiration. My hope was that his genius would take off as if he were at work on canvas or stone. I saw my role as making certain that these two operas would, in fact, inspire him, advising him of the practical demands of the theater, scene by scene. I also had to insure that what he was proposing was going to work and that the operas would not be submerged in the designs.

Normally the director is supreme arbiter of all questions about what is seen and done, but when you invite someone like David Hockney to team up with you, you know you will surrender much of your autonomy. A small price to pay, as it turned out.

Once Hockney was persuaded that his lack of theatrical experience was no handicap—it was his inventiveness that initially attracted Glyndebourne—he and Cox set about determining the look of *The Rake*. The 18th-century engraving technique of William Hogarth, with its wealth of descriptive detail, offered endless ideas and Cox says he was enthusiastic about Hockney's first proposal which was predicated on these images.

When he came back with the crosshatching idea, using the restricted palette and thus making it very much his own, I was delighted because the idea was so musically correct. Being a 20th-century utilization of an 18th-century technique, it coincided exactly with the sources of Stravinsky's own musical inspiration. In a way, it was even more exact, for Stravinsky's harmonies have an acid-etched quality, yet the first idea for the opera came from Hogarth's oil paintings of A Rake's Progress, *not the engravings. Once I had accepted this style—it took a microsecond!—it was thereafter a matter of describing to David the action, content and mood of each scene, and asking him to match them, detail for detail, from the whole corpus of Hogarth's work.*

From the start, Cox wanted the sets to function symbolically as well as descriptively. The benighted hero, Tom Rakewell, having made his pact with the devil in the person of Nick Shadow, would be raised to dizzying heights of

Trulove's Garden
model for *The Rake's Progress*   1975
ink on cardboard
16 × 21 × 12

Brothel Scene from *The Rake's Progress*
as performed at Glyndebourne Festival Opera, 1975
Tom Rakewell: Leo Goeke
Mother Goose: Thetis Blacker
Nick Shadow: Donald Gramm

Bedlam Scene from *The Rake's Progress*
as performed at Glyndebourne Festival Opera, 1975
Tom Rakewell: Leo Goeke
Anne Trulove: Jill Gomez
and members of the Glyndebourne Festival Opera Chorus

(p 82)
Tom's Room (Room 1)
model for *The Rake's Progress*   1975
ink on cardboard
16 × 21 × 12

Tom's Room with Baba's Hanging Objects
model for *The Rake's Progress*   1975
ink on cardboard
16 × 21 × 12

(p 83)
Tom's Room, Auction Scene
model for *The Rake's Progress*   1975
ink on cardboard
16 × 21 × 12

Bedlam
model for *The Rake's Progress*   1975
ink on cardboard
16 × 21 × 12

wealth and social status, and experience in full measure the joys of the flesh before his inevitable decline. Cox and Hockney were agreed that each scene should reflect another step of Tom's steady descent. In the opening scene, which takes place in a garden where Tom Rakewell and Nick Shadow meet, Cox wanted to make certain the audience got the message that Tom's fate was already determined.

My first request to David was that it should be a walled garden with a solid door. In an artless way it should be a prison for Tom. He should be unable to open the door, because he lacks willpower. (Only Nick and Anne Trulove,* Tom's betrothed, representing opposite poles of evil and good, are ever seen to open it.) Otherwise, the only idea I contributed was the swing. The musical accompaniment to Anne's first words sounds a bit like a creaky swing, and there is innocence in the image. David very wittily saw the potential corruption in it too, and wanted a couple of whores on swings in the subsequent brothel scene, but there were practical problems—not the lack of underwear, but the lack of swinging space in a crowded fly-gallery!

Cox felt there should be strong and cohesive visual elements in two of the opera's most spectacular scenes, one in the brothel where Tom receives his vivid sexual initiation from Mother Goose herself, the other in Bedlam which occurs at the close of the opera where he has been robbed of his reason by Nick Shadow. So overpowering are the dramatic action and music in both scenes, that Cox wanted to contain them within a strong, centralized design.

For the brothel scene I wanted to assure a strong visual focus. It's a scene which, like Bedlam, can go out of control, so I suggested a large double bed as a "throne" for Mother Goose. I also felt very strongly that there is no eroticism in the music, just a perverted innocence which has a delicious naiveté all its own, with catechism and folk song verging on nursery rhyme. I was also anxious that the scene should somehow be a counterpart to Bedlam, because in the first Tom loses his innocence and in the second, he regains it.

In the brothel scene, Hockney came up with an ingenious solution to the moral paradox in which innocence and "experience" coexisted. One of its prominent features was the series of small rooms to which the prostitutes led their clients. These were virtually toy cupboards where, Cox says, "the couples retired, so to speak, to play with their toys." Hockney's cellular design of people in boxes was repeated, in distorted perspective, in the culminating Bedlam scene.

The three scenes of Tom's London townhouse morning room were entirely Hockney's idea. In each set the room assumes a different identity. The first reveals the room in all its elegance, indicating that Tom Rakewell is well on

*Anne's family name has been spelled in one of two ways in previous publications: Trulove in the Earl of Harewood's *The New Kobbé's Complete Opera Book* (New York: G. P. Putnam's Sons, 1976), and in the *Glyndebourne Festival Programme Book 1975* (Lewes: Glyndebourne Festival Opera, 1975); and Truelove in the opera libretto for *The Rake's Progress* by W. H. Auden and Chester Kallman (New York: Boosey & Hawkes, 1951).

Leave all love and hope behind

out of sight is out of mind

Graveyard
model for *The Rake's Progress*   1975
ink on cardboard
16 × 21 × 12

his way to the fame and fortune promised him by Shadow. Hockney decided that Tom's sudden rise to affluence and social status would best be exemplified by making him a compulsive art collector. In the second set, the room is drastically transformed to a repository for Baba the Turk's collection of exotic junk and takes on surreal character; among her bizarre trophies from innumerable admirers are stuffed animals, birds, snuff boxes, fossils, Roman busts. Cox marvels at Hockney's capacity to invest the same interior with varying moods.

> *The third room scene, all in black and white, is the most bravura of all visually and certainly elicited from me the most bravura direction. David said here that as Tom's misfortunes increase, so color departs, and this made splendid sense.*

In the graveyard scene, Shadow at last claims his wages, the heavy price of Tom's year and a day of freedom and profligacy, and the miserable hero is given his choice of ways to die. Hockney decided that the graveyard scene should be all in black; in fact, as Cox observes, the cardboard walls of the model Hockney made for this set were painted black and he used a scraping technique to indicate details of the design in white. It was, Cox says, a complete "negative." Tom and Shadow play at cards, with Tom's soul the prize. The inspiration for this ominous tableau, Cox says, was

> *a Hogarth of two figures playing cards on a tomb—and re-creating this was a must. Again, as with the bed in the brothel, a large object, the tomb, gave sharp focus to a scene, and gave the character, Nick Shadow, a chance to play at theater a bit.*

Though Tom, by recalling the tender feelings he once had for Anne Trulove, manages to win the card game and thus save his life, Shadow's revenge is to render him insane. The poignancy of this situation is given full rein in the final Bedlam scene where Tom, robbed of his reason and thinking himself to be Adonis, pines for his lost love, Anne, whom he calls Venus. For this vividly dramatic scene the dominant stage element is a large, crate-like structure from whose rectangular compartments a masked chorus rises and holds forth sorrowfully. This design idea, we learn, developed from a more modest scheme.

> *As an early idea for this scene, David showed me three or four characters in boxes. I suggested we should put the entire chorus in boxes. This was the happiest collaborative coup of all, for I hated the prospect of the singers doing their own thing in that awful Actors Studio way of representing madness of all kinds (e.g., Marat-Sade and We Come to the River). This way, we could use the chorus as figments of Tom's diseased imagination. Again, it was a question of controlling the focus, and here it always had to be on Tom. We had already included his bed as a direct reminder of the Brothel (catechism on the latter to Mother Goose; final confession here to Anne). The "boxed" chorus completed this reference to that scene and was, incidentally, the only other scene that got off floor level.*

With *The Rake*, both Hockney and Cox were working from similar 18th-

William Hogarth
*The Idle 'Prentice at Play in the Church Yard,
During Divine Service*
from *Industry and Idleness*   1747
engraving
10 × 13⅜

century visual conventions and the production style was easily set at the start. *The Magic Flute*, on the other hand, offered no such hard and fast visual precedents and to a great extent each man went his own way. To complicate matters, Hockney was working in New York and Cox in Australia.

The collaboration was more difficult and, in the end, perhaps led to a less satisfactory result theatrically—this in spite of the fact that Hockney created several stage pictures of great beauty. One of the problems was that we were not very much together during the creative process—much less than in The Rake, *so that I was unable to do a theatrical monitoring job. Knowing that we were going to be working in absentia, I wrote a long scenic analysis for David's guidance, describing my ideas as they were at the outset, but this was only of limited value to him, because no real dialogue could take place. By the time I saw the designs in New York it was too late because of deadlines, to ask him to reconsider anything very radically, so I realized then that I would have to people "his"* Flute *rather than direct "ours."*

The designs I saw in the model were strong, striking and vivid explosions of color, especially after the austerity of The Rake. *There was a farrago of influences, borrowings and sly cross references to so many parts of art history, but this in itself did not worry me. The Flute is equally multifarious, and in my view, the only available unity for it was the unity of diversity. Many aspects of David's own work seemed to single him out as just the right artist to impose his style on this work, and so much of the Hockney iconography can indeed be found in these designs. Besides, both of our theatrical roots are firmly embedded in the popular theater of the English provinces, his in Bradford, mine in Bristol— namely, Christmas pantomimes in which short scenes of comparable diversity are strung together on a loose, narrative thread, with no regard for tight organic development or consistency of style. That is to say, variety is the guiding principle, and it clearly was also David's. This reference back to pantomime was, I am sure, justified. (Indeed, we even incorporated the principle of the double- manned pantomime horse into the scene of the enchanted animals.) Our adherence to its freedoms ensured a highly entertaining* Flute, *but perhaps rather at the expense of the sublime.*

Having designed a series of static tableaux for Rake, *David was anxious to use the instrument of the theater with more resource, albeit traditionally, making sure, meanwhile, that there would be no waiting between scenes. Far from being jaded by, or contemptuous of, such a simple business as flying painted cloths up and down, he revelled in it and considered its effect miraculous, which it is. Similarly, the dissolving of a scene through a scrim can have sheer magic qualities and this was exploited in Act I, Scene I, as Uccello's landscape melted away to become a starry empyrean for the Queen's appearance. Once seen, however, the stars stubbornly refused to vanish completely as required, and this was the first indication of the tiresome troubles which dogged the technical realization of the design, for in Glyndebourne's crowded fly-gallery it was not possible to separate the two flown cloths*

leave out beard
for
papagena

the tail is part
of the cage.
it could fold up
when he takes
cage off.

papageno

sufficiently. And as in other scenes, the modern lighting equipment was, ironically, unable to light the work really well—that is to say, as pictures.

Cox still has mixed emotions about the outcome of the collaboration on *The Magic Flute*. While he was fascinated by the freshness and originality of Hockney's sets, his problem was to make these radiant enclosures support the opera's action. It was frequently necessary to improvise solutions to allow characters to go about their business. For example, he says the apartment in Sarastro's palace in which the heroine, Pamina, is imprisoned

. . . suffered most from my lack of contact with David during designing. In the model it looked well enough, but had no provision for entry and exit and no sense of her captivity—benign or otherwise. The scene was saved quite fortuitously by the use of a trap in the Glyndebourne stage which enabled Papageno to do a relatively convincing excavated break-in, and to dispatch Monostatos by the same route.

Cox realized that Glyndebourne's small stage prevented Hockney from fully realizing his fantasies about *The Magic Flute*. Deep space had to be achieved through illusion, foreshortening and other perspectival devices of which Hockney was a master. His conception of the environs of Sarastro's kingdom, Cox says, was of "a superb vista, kibbutz-like on the edge of the desert. One saw at once the utopian quality of Sarastro's realm."

Sadly, in order to expose this to view, the city walls which should confront Tamino had to be dispensed with, leaving three small doors instead of temple portals, and no majesty or authority of architecture. I was anxious to show what a desirable place Sarastro's realm must be—one has no real chance later—and gave David the doomed task of reconciling impossibles.

The several scenes of Act II, most of which occur within the temple's precincts, its gardens and mysterious vaults, were altogether more successful. They were full of bold, rich color, strong geometry and brilliant tricks of perspective.

Improvisation seemed to have been the rule during many aspects of *The Flute* production, often with fortuitous results.

The scenes changed rapidly, if not always by the most orthodox means. (I remember the garden wall in Papageno's suicide scene being held up by six unflinching stage crew crouching out of sight.) The lighting was more effective, being atmospheric and nocturnal, and spatially the acting area waxed and waned with a satisfying rhythm.

All things considered, the most effective scenes were those in which the action and the painted cloths were confined far downstage, carefully lit from the front, and the whole aspired most nearly to the nature of a picture in a frame. David's conquest of space was still to come.

The most unsatisfactory aspect of our Magic Flute *was the costumes, where David's eclecticism fell short of perfection because it became difficult for him to know where to turn. We had from the start rejected the Druidical look for the priests—David derided the Mormon Tabernacle Choir look, and I*

Papageno
sketch for *The Magic Flute*   1978
ink on paper
17 × 14

wanted the sense of people working with their hands and brains to build a utopia rather than simply praying it into existence. Yet we were in an exotic world, western eyes looking east, and finished up with a hybrid and not very wearable Assyrian look. Some of the principals' costumes, too, had a curiously muted impact and were perhaps in the wrong fabrics, besides. David was very unhappy about them and often regretted that he had had to let the set model go before designing them. He was designing the costumes in a void, and one wonders, say, if he would have chosen to copy the Schinkel design for the Queen of the Night and the traditional feathered suit for Papageno had he had their environments before him as he worked.

Though Cox and Hockney seemed to diverge at various points in their conceptions of *The Magic Flute*, they were agreed on treating the opera as a wondrous, utopian world where virtue triumphs over evil. Cox, who saw *The Flute* as an earthy morality play, ponders his approach to it.

I think the emphasis on the human content of Magic Flute *at the expense of the sublime was the result of my wanting to present its world very much through the eyes of Papageno. I didn't really want him to be a feathered creature like some overgrown Peter Pan, but in the end I let it go because the first Papageno, Ben Luxon, had all the right qualities of maturity and masculinity! The absurdity of such a costume on such a man had positive benefits, emphasizing his enforced lack of fulfillment, slavery almost. He is a type of Everyman: the humble, worthy fellow without whom the great could never be great, but who has to do all the dirty, dangerous work in order to get them there. We are never quite sure what Tamino really stands for in the end. What is, after all, this generalized princely virtue he symbolizes? Papageno, however, we can really get to know.*

In their productions of *The Rake's Progress* and *The Magic Flute*, Cox and Hockney made frequent allusions to the spirit of the 18th century. Both heroes, Rakewell and Tamino, make their initial appearances as innocents. *The Rake* is ultimately a pessimistic tale of lost innocence and corruption whose protagonist, in his eagerness to achieve wealth and fame, abandons Anne, his true love, and makes a pact with the devil. Rakewell follows his destiny through crosshatched Hogarthian vignettes of gardens, streets and, finally, to the madhouse. His "progress," however, is a descent through layers of degradation and only in his final uncomprehending state, does he regain his innocence. *The Magic Flute*, despite its pairings of appropriately suited lovers, is about the attainment of higher goals. Tamino, wandering in dream-like landscapes reminiscent of ancient Egypt, pursues wisdom, nature and reason. He ennobles himself spiritually and finds true love in the bargain. The leading characters in the Stravinsky and Mozart operas symbolize two opposing views of life, which the direction and design of both productions strongly emphasized.

David Hockney seated in front of an element of *The Magic Flute's* rocky landscape set from Act 1, 1978.

The Rake's Progress

as told by David Hockney

Production series from *The Rake's Progress*, as performed by the San Francisco Opera, June 1982. Conductor: David Agler, Stage Director: John Cox, Lighting: Joan Sullivan; and the cast featured Anne Trulove: Diane Soviero, Tom Rakewell: Dennis Bailey, Father Trulove: Kevin Langan, Nick Shadow: Donald Gramm, Mother Goose: Regina Sarfaty, Baba the Turk: Mignon Dumm, Sellem: Jonathan Green, Keeper of the Madhouse: Gregory Stapp.

(1) Tom Rakewell is engaged to Anne Trulove, the daughter of Father Trulove. They live in domestic tranquility in the country. You have no idea of the size of their house, though in the stage directions it seems to be located in the corner of a garden. Tom seems very innocent, placid—that's your first impression. Father Trulove decides to speak to Tom about his future and suggests to Anne that her advice is needed in the kitchen. Anne replies—as she does throughout the opera—"Yes, father," and departs.

(2) Her father tells Tom he has arranged a clerical job for him in the city of London and then he leaves Tom alone in the garden. Tom is not thrilled at that prospect and declares (and I think the libretto borrowed this from Martin Luther), "Here I stand, my constitution sound," which suggests he has other ambitions. At the end of his speech he says: "I wish I had money!" And standing at the garden gate is a mysterious-looking character in black, none other than the Devil, Nick Shadow.

(3) Shadow says he is looking for Tom Rakewell to tell him that an uncle, who had left England many years before, has died and left him a legacy. Tom says, "My parents never mentioned one." "They quarreled, I believe, sir," Nick replies. "You are a rich man." Just like that! So Tom's wish seems to have been granted.

(4) Father Trulove is quite pleased and encourages Tom to go to London to put his affairs in order. Off they go, Tom Rakewell and Nick Shadow, to receive the fortune, and at the end of the scene Shadow says, "The progress of a rake begins."

(7) When scene three begins, we return to the Truloves' garden. Anne is very worried about Tom who has been away for quite a while now, and she doesn't know what to do. She decides to find him in London and leaves surreptitiously at night.

(8) Act II begins in the morning room of Tom's fine London house. From the look of things, he's been spending lots of money. There's been a game of cards going on, but Tom is getting a little bored these days—there's something lacking in his life.

(5) The next scene is Mother Goose's Brothel in London, filled with whores and roaring boys surrounding Mother Goose, who wishes to initiate Tom herself. Nick Shadow, as we see, is introducing Tom to the finer things of life, the delights of London.

(6) In the brothel, Tom is asked wonderful questions: "What is Pleasure, then?" He replies, "The idol of all dreams, the same / Whatever shape it wear or name; / Whom flirts imagine as a hat / Old maids believe to be a cat." When he is asked what love is, he replies, "That precious word is like a fiery coal / It burns my lips, strikes terror to my soul." But he does not really answer the question.

(9) Nick Shadow appears and asks him if he's been to St. Giles Fair to see Baba the Turk. Tom says he has not, ". . . brave warriors . . . have swooned after a mere glimpse of her." Nick then shows Tom a picture of Baba and asks, "Do you desire her?" Tom replies, "Like the gout or the falling sickness."

(10) Here, the story gets into a philosophical point. Shadow persuades Tom to exercise his free will and do something he knows he shouldn't. He tells him to ignore those "twin tyrants of appetite and conscience" and to marry Baba the Turk. So, taking up the challenge, Tom not only marries the bearded lady, but brings her and her great collection of exotic objects to his house.

(11) In a rather grand scene, Baba arrives in a sedan chair, with all the people from the street coming to look at her.

(12) Meanwhile, Anne has found her way to Tom's house and watches the grand procession. Suddenly, she sees Tom who greets her gently and also tells her to flee London for the country. The city is a bad place. Baba the Turk sits and waits and finally, impatiently asks, ". . . am I to remain in here forever?" Anne asks who she is and Tom says, "My wife. . ." Anne says, "I see, then it is I who was unworthy," and leaves, brokenhearted. When Baba the Turk asks, "Who was that girl?" Tom says, "Only a milkmaid, pet / To whom I was in debt."

(15) At the beginning of Act III, which takes place in Tom's house, all the objects in Baba's collection are being auctioned off. While the auction is going on, Anne Trulove arrives and asks where Tom is. The chorus of Respectable Citizens tells her all kinds of things: He's gone off to America; "Spontaneous combustion caught him hurrying." He's dead.

(16) As the auction proceeds, Sellem, the auctioneer, points to something hidden under the tablecloth. (It's Baba, still covered with the cloth Tom angrily threw over her.) "And now for the truly adventurous," he says, and everyone starts bidding excitedly.

(13) Next, Baba the Turk and Tom are shut in the morning room together, and Baba just does not stop talking. She sings that marvelous chatterbox aria about the gifts her many admirers have bestowed upon her. Tom is not amused. In fact, he is bored again. He knows something is missing from his life. Baba is annoyed and starts smashing Tom's crockery. He throws a tablecloth over Baba to silence her, then falls asleep—there's nothing left for him to do but sleep.

(14) Now, Nick Shadow wheels a strange contraption into the room. When Tom wakes up, he says he's had a dream about a machine that can turn stone into bread, whereupon Nick Shadow shows him what he has brought. The audience sees that it's obviously a fake, but Tom is gullible enough to fall for it. Tom is excited by the bread machine, especially since his money has been used up. When he and Nick Shadow go off with the bread machine to raise money in the city, it's the last we see of Tom for a while.

(17) Suddenly, he lifts the cloth and Baba, indignant, tells him the sale is over. In the crowd she recognizes Anne whom she realizes is still in love with Tom, and that theirs is a "true love." She tells Anne to find Tom, that he's out there somewhere, wretched.

(18) The next scene is in a graveyard where Nick Shadow has taken Tom a year and a day after they met. You realize that the Devil wants to be paid for his services. It's Tom's soul that Shadow wants. Tom, who is terrified, cries, "Have mercy on me, Heaven!" And Nick Shadow, being a gambler, says, "Very well then . . . A game of chance to decide your fate. Have you a pack of cards?"

(19) They play, and with each card Tom miraculously receives a clue. Thinking of Anne Trulove, he correctly guesses that the first card is the Queen of Hearts. When a spade, leaning against a grave, falls over, Tom cries out, "The deuce!" And seeing what fell, he says "the two of spades." Then Nick Shadow tries to cheat and slips the Queen of Hearts back into the pack as the third card. Poor Tom, still unable to think of anything else but Anne, says, "O Queen of Hearts, again," and he wrestles the card from Nick Shadow's hand, thus winning the game.

(20) Shadow, furious, admits defeat but says to Tom, "Henceforth be you insane!" and disappears into the grave. The last scene is in Bedlam, the insane asylum. Anne has been told by the jailer that Tom believes himself to be Adonis, so she goes along with the idea that she is Venus. They sing together very tenderly.

(21) Finally, Father Trulove comes to find Anne, to tell her that the story has ended and she must go home. Once again Anne says, "Yes, Father," and they exit, leaving Tom in the madhouse.

(22) Just as the opera is about to end, the main characters come out and as the audience starts to applaud, they raise their hands and say, "Good people, just a moment / Though our story now is ended / There's the moral to draw / From what you saw / Since the curtain first ascended." The moral is that the Devil makes work for idle hands. And that's the end of the opera.

Designing
The Rake's Progress

Martin Friedman and David Hockney

If Glyndebourne's invitation to design *The Rake's Progress* had not come when it did in the summer of 1974, Hockney's subsequent development as a painter might have been different, indeed. At that time, he was perfecting a drawing style, equal parts idealization and observation. In place of the spontaneity of the 1960s his work had by then assumed a measured, quasi-official character. For Hockney, the 1970s was a time of elegant portraits in colored pencil, crayon and ink of close friends such as Henry Geldzahler, Gregory Evans, Celia Birtwell, Peter Schlesinger, Nick Wilder, Mark Lancaster and of his parents. It was also a period of such stately large-scale double portraits as *Mr. and Mrs. Clark and Percy,* 1970-71 (Ossie Clark and Celia Birtwell and their cat), *Gregory Masurovsky and Shirley Goldfarb,* 1974, and *George Lawson and Wayne Sleep,* 1975. No accidental effects were admitted in those hermetic compositions, with figures posed in studied relationship to one another and to their sparse surroundings. For all their subtle modeling in light and shadow, these people were strangely weightless beings. Hockney only hints at volume in these static, Ingres-like tableaux whose characters exist in a flat continuum of mirage-like surfaces.

Hockney recalls the exasperation of his London dealer, John Kasmin, who, visiting him in Paris, urged that he abandon his unrelenting academicism and return to a free approach. But so determined was the artist to master descriptive drawing that, by his own admission, he had trapped himself in the pursuit of technique.

At that time I had not been doing much painting because I was trying to teach myself to draw better. I would spend two or three days working on a figure, scrutinizing it carefully. I thought this would improve my drawing because my eyes would see more.

Even before Glyndebourne wrote to him, Hockney had been casting about for alternatives to his compulsive drawing style. As matters turned out, *The Rake's Progress* would be the vehicle for his release. Though at first reluctant to consider the project seriously because he had no experience in opera

Kerby (After Hogarth) Useful Knowledge 1975
oil on canvas
72 × 60⅛
Collection The Museum of Modern Art, New York
Gift of the artist, John Kasmin and Advisory Committee Fund

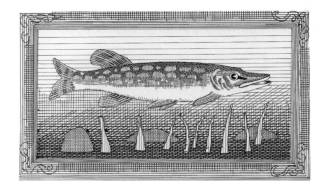

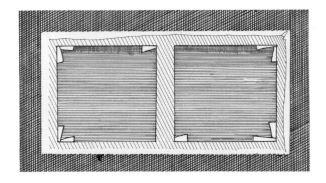

Front and Back of Painting of a Pike
sketches for *The Rake's Progress*   1975
ink on paper
7 × 11 each

Baba, Red Pantaloons
sketch for *The Rake's Progress*   1975
ink on paper
17 × 14

production, he agreed to talk things over with the Glyndebourne staff.

I had only a general idea of what an opera production might involve. I knew those at Covent Garden were usually more costly than ordinary theater productions. The only thing I had done in the theater, Ubu Roi, was very simply conceived, because it suited the work. Even though I told the Glyndebourne people I didn't really think I knew enough to do the job, they convinced me I did.

I realized they expected me simply to make eight or nine drawings of the scenes and hand them over. They would then interpret these and make them into sets. So I started making a few drawings.

On the advice of a friend, Mo MacDermott, Hockney decided to make his designs as detailed as possible, leaving nothing to chance. Though eight years earlier he had provided the Royal Court Theatre with a set of drawings for *Ubu Roi*, Glyndebourne's requirements, he decided, posed more complicated problems.

Mo, who worked for me then a bit, had also worked for a stage designer in London. He told me not just to do drawings because the result on stage might not look exactly as I wanted it to. I realized that working with something as stylized as opera, you must control how everything looks. You must design the production in three dimensions. I decided to make scale models of the sets.

Hockney had long been fascinated by Hogarth's engravings on the Rake theme and those for *Marriage à la Mode*. Intrigued with the precision of the crosshatching technique so prominent in these prints, he decided to apply similar patterning in exaggerated scale to all architectural elements and costumes in the production. That style was particularly expressive, he felt, of the jagged, linear character of Stravinsky's music. Using the hallmark of 18th-century engraving was consistent with the composer's own concept of the production. Stravinsky's music, Hockney says, "was a pastiche of Mozart's, and my design was a pastiche of Hogarth's."

The misadventures of the Rake, Hockney reminds us, have no literary ancestry; we know it through Hogarth's eyes.

It was never a written story. It is a tale that you deduce from his images. Auden and Kallman based their libretto on Hogarth's scenario but added many twists of their own. In Hogarth's version, for instance, Tom marries an ugly old maid when the money runs out. Instead of an ugly lady, Auden and Kallman decided to bring in a bearded lady, Baba the Turk.

Hockney was no stranger to Hogarth's work, and in the early 1960s even did a suite of prints loosely predicated on the Rake theme.

To any English art student, William Hogarth is a great artist. It always seemed to me that he had a very human eye. He understood mankind's follies and had a soft spot for them, but his work also shows a certain delight in condemning low life.

For his *Rake's Progress* series, Hockney made sixteen two-color prints, using a technique combining etching and aquatint. The idea for these came

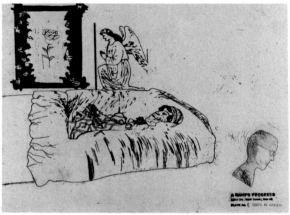

Meeting the Good People (Washington)

Death in Harlem

Bedlam

from A Rake's Progress 1961–63
etching and aquatint on paper
12 × 16 each

from his first visit to New York in 1961. With its startling extremes of wealth and squalor, the city seemed the perfect setting for a morality tale, with himself in the role of benighted hero.

What struck me about New York was the experience of walking on the Bowery and seeing drunks lying about in the street. Frankly, in the English welfare state, you didn't see that. But I thought the derelicts in New York were just like those in Hogarth's London. When, a year or so later I looked at his engravings for A Rake's Progress I thought, well, you could do a modern version of this. Originally I was just going to do eight etchings using the same sequences that Hogarth did, but in the end I made sixteen.

When the Rake is first seen in my prints, he is a vivid personality, but little by little he loses this quality. For the last scene, in Bedlam, I did a drawing of a faceless figure, then made a stamp of it that I impressed on the etching plate five times. You see five faceless people in the madhouse, but you can't tell which one the Rake is. They all wear T-shirts that say, "I swing with WABC" and have little radios plugged into their ears. Before that time I'd never seen radios like those; they didn't exist in Europe. At first, I thought they were hearing aids; I thought some disease had struck the young of New York.

In his Rake prints, Hockney used a naive, near-cartoon style that lends itself admirably to their themes of degradation and dehumanization. Even though some episodes, according to their titles, occur in Harlem, Madison Square Garden and Washington, D.C., there is little sense of time or place in these Kafkaesque visions. In successive scenes, the young man yields to temptations, succumbs to frightful mishaps and is soon reduced to non-person status.

In contrast to this extremely subjective conception of the Rake theme, Hockney's designs for Glyndebourne were hard-edged, finely detailed and calculated to enhance every aspect of the story. He knew his job was to provide a coherent visual context for the action and, to that end, analyzed the Auden/Kallman text, scene by scene. He quickly incorporated his ideas into models which he conceived of as three-dimensional drawings. He recalls showing these for the first time to the Glyndebourne staff in London.

Everyone who was going to be involved with the production was there—the producers, the prop people, the lighting man. They were totally amazed when they saw the designs. They were expecting to see drawings, but I had made a model for almost every set. What I didn't know at the time was that some of them thought my ideas wouldn't work. I later learned that some thought crosshatching the entire set was too much—they thought it was a mad idea, but didn't say anything. I was concerned about the crosshatching, too, so I decided to go to Glyndebourne and test my idea. We made lots of samples of crosshatchings in different sizes, and hung them up on the stage. I sat at the back of the theater with binoculars, deciding what the scale should be. If it was done too small, it would look like a solid color. If it was too big, it would look like a checkerboard—and that would be ridiculous. So I made some calculations and came up with the exact size.

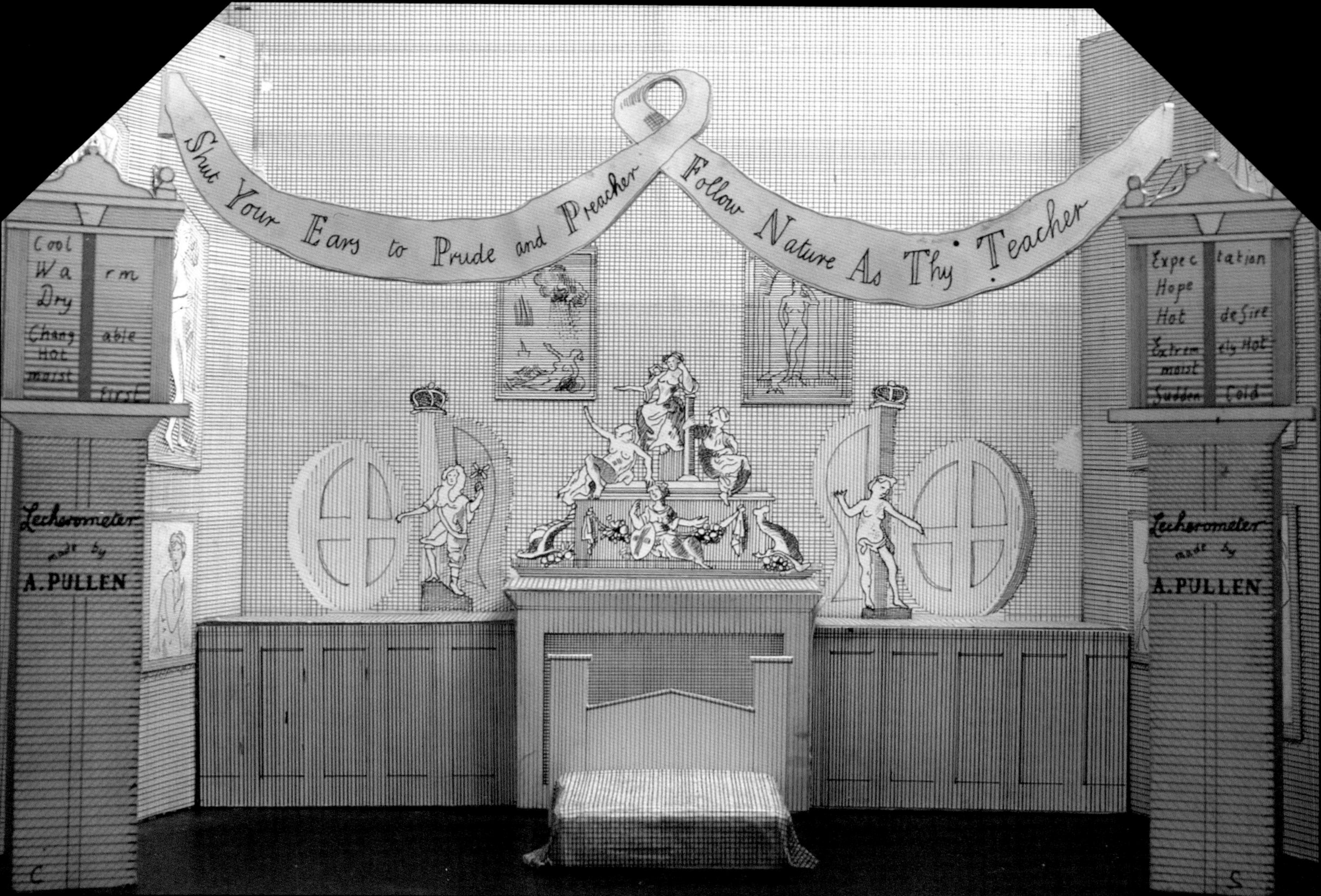

Shut Your Ears to Pride and Preacher · Follow Nature As Thy Teacher

Cool
Wa   rm
Dry
Chang   able
Hot
moist
            first

Lectorometer
made by
A. PULLEN

Expec   tation
Hope
Hot   desire
Extreme ly Hot
moist
Sudden   Cold

Lectorometer
made by
A. PULLEN

C

S

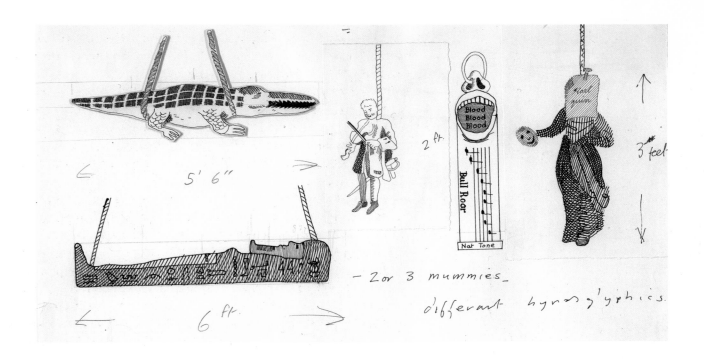

Baba's Hanging Objects
sketch for *The Rake's Progress*   1975
ink on paper
12 × 16

He presented the Glyndebourne people with a number of set designs, executed in colored inks, each symmetrically composed in one-point perspective.

> I think I arrived at the color for the sets this way. Crosshatching is a graphic technique that normally is done with a single color. But then, I thought, we don't want to do it all in black and white. We have to use some colored lines; so I simply chose what would have been standard printing colors in the 18th century. I bought good German inks; red, blue, green and black. There are no other colors in the design. I used colors in The Rake mainly as decorative elements. They are essentially tints.

Though Hogarth's engravings were the most pervasive influence on Hockney's *Rake* designs, more subliminal forces were at work. His consuming interest in museum collections of all sorts is reflected ironically in the bizarre group of objects he has provided Baba the Turk. Though Tom's wildly transformed house is strongly reminiscent of Hogarth's treatment of that scene, Hockney has approached its design with glee and ingenuity. Crowding the shelves, covering the walls and hanging from the ceiling of poor Rakewell's morning room are such wonders as a sphinx, a giant snail shell, assorted fossils and the mummified crocodile. There is a conspicuous analogy to Pop Art: Hockney's enlarged crosshatching throughout *The Rake* generates an optical vibrato similar to that of the benday dot patterns in Roy Lichtenstein's paintings.

Indeed, the overwhelming impression of *The Rake* on stage is oscillating line. Sometimes Hockney's fluent line models a chair leg, a cabinet of knick-

(p 103)
Mother Goose's Brothel
model for *The Rake's Progress*   1975
ink on cardboard
16 × 21 × 12

104

knacks, a window detail or a room corner; other times it careens about like automatic writing, an example being the feverish scrawls on the opening curtain and the graffiti on the madhouse walls.

Where do you think I got the idea to use graffiti in the Bedlam scene? From Hogarth again, of course. I suddenly realized that in his Bedlam drawing, one of the madmen is scribbling a map of the world on the wall. Then I thought about what the walls of Bedlam must have been covered with and decided that in the 18th century the graffiti wouldn't have been political; probably it was mostly intellectual.

Although the freedom of working on the Stravinsky opera broke academicism's hold on Hockney and encouraged him to draw more adventurously again, only one painting has its direct ancestry in *The Rake* project. In *Kerby (After Hogarth) Useful Knowledge,** Hockney again made wry and respectful reference to his distant mentor. During his research on 18th-century drawing techniques, he had come across John Kirby's classic manual on the art of perspective and marveled at its frontispiece by Hogarth—a festival of spatial incongruities. Hockney's *Kerby*, begun in the spring of 1975, like the Hogarth drawing, seems at first to be a more or less normal depiction of a landscape, complete with river, house and a few fishermen. This, of course, turns out to be a completely erroneous reading, since Hockney has incorporated as many violations of the rules as he could manage. There is no single vanishing point, nor do parallel lines meet in the distance—rather, they go off in opposite directions. Objects in the foreground and background illogically occupy the same space: a sign suspended from a house in the foreground rests behind a row of trees far away.

Kerby represents an important summation of ideas that preoccupied Hockney during the design of *The Rake*. Its red, green and blue tonality echoes that of the opera. The engraving analogy is carried further in rows of thin parallel lines that define the painting's water and sky areas. These contrast sharply with the planar, earth-colored masses of the house, whose volumes, shown in arbitrary perspective, resemble a cubistic configuration. At one point he had considered using Hogarth's irrational perspective as the basis for the opera design, but later settled for applying these non-rules to a large painting.

Hockney's *Kerby* is a prophetic work in many ways. The sculptured hill and tree growing from it would have their incarnations in *The Magic Flute* sets; the brick pattern of the ruined bridge over the river anticipated the endless rows of bricks in *The Flute*'s huge pyramid. But perhaps the most important thing about *Kerby* for Hockney's future work was the way he dealt with space in this painting; it is understood in purely subjective terms, suspending all rules of illusionistic perspective in the process.

Cover for the program of *The Rake's Progress*, Glyndebourne Festival Opera 1975
offset lithography on paper
12¼ × 9½

*John Kirby (1716–1774) was an English artist and author of *Architectural Perspective*. Hockney's reference to him in the title of his painting *Kerby (After Hogarth) Useful Knowledge* uses a different spelling of the 18th-century artist's family name.

The Magic Flute

as told by David Hockney

Production series from *The Magic Flute*, as performed at Glyndebourne Festival Opera, 1978. (See Opera Chart, p 216) Tamino: Leo Goeke, Papageno: Benjamin Luxon, Queen of the Night: May Sandoz, Pamina: Isobel Buchanan, Sarastro: Thomas Thomaschke, Papagena: Elizabeth Couquet.

(1) There's a Prince, Tamino, who is wandering around Egypt dressed in a hunting costume. A monster, a dragon, comes to attack him. He faints in fear of the monster and is rescued by Three Ladies who kill the beast.

(2) When he wakes up, Papageno, Mr. Everyman, has arrived. Papageno, a rather jovial, easy-going character who is dressed in brightly-colored feathers, catches birds for the Queen of the Night. He claims he killed the monster with both hands.

(3) At this point, the Three Ladies come back and say, "Papageno, that is naughty of you. You shouldn't tell lies." And they put a lock on his mouth. They tell the Prince that it was they who killed the monster and all three of them fall in love with him. They tell him he is in the kingdom of the Queen of the Night. The Three Ladies give Prince Tamino a picture of the Queen's daughter, and he immediately falls in love with the girl in the picture. He sings a wonderful aria about how beautiful she is.

(4) The Queen appears and tells Prince Tamino that her daughter, Pamina, has been kidnapped by a wicked man, Sarastro, and asks if he would go and rescue her. The Three Ladies give him a magic flute to help him in case he comes into danger.

(7) The Prince, who has found Sarastro's kingdom and its temples of Wisdom, Reason and Nature, is suspicious, because what he discovers doesn't quite tie in with what the Queen of the Night told him about Sarastro's being such a wicked man. In fact, it does look as if there is some sense of order in Sarastro's place and nothing at all that looks evil. At one point, the Prince plays the magic flute, which brings wild beasts, charmed and made peaceable by the music, to surround him. (Tenors, I'm told, do not like this scene much as the animals can upstage their singing.)

(8) Papageno gets a chance to use his magic bells when he and Pamina are recaptured by Monostatos. The bells have the effect of tranquilizing his captors and making them dance off the stage. After a lot of confusion, the three travelers are captured and finally meet in Sarastro's kingdom. Sarastro tells the Princess he has rescued her from her mother, the Queen of the Night, who he says is really the evil one. Then Prince Tamino is told he is now among an important order of priests and, if he wishes, he can join this brotherhood by undergoing certain rites of passage and purification.

(5) They suggest that Papageno go with him, but Papageno resists, as he's afraid of Sarastro. He agrees to accompany Tamino only after the Three Ladies give him his own lucky charm—a set of magic bells.

(6) In the next scene, the Princess is the prisoner of the slave, Monostatos; but Papageno rescues her when Monostatos, frightened by Papageno, runs off to ask for help, leaving Papageno and Pamina free to go. Papageno tells Pamina of Tamino's love for her and she is eager to meet him.

(9) Act II begins with Sarastro and his followers singing beautiful music. That's the bit that George Bernard Shaw said was ". . . probably the nearest music ever came to God's voice. If God ever sang it would be like this." Act II is about the long journey and trials that the two couples, Tamino and Pamina and Papageno and Papagena (still to appear) must endure. The high priest Sarastro and his followers agree to allow Tamino to join their brotherhood. Tamino tells them he's a Prince and is willing to undergo any ordeal to win Pamina.

(10) Papageno is dragged along. They begin the journey in a very dark place, just outside the temple. They have taken a vow of silence, but of course Papageno immediately wants to break it. He's perfectly willing to go back to his quiet life as a bird-catcher for the town, but he can't escape and agrees to go when he is promised a wife as a reward. The Queen of the Night sends the Three Ladies who earlier rescued Tamino from the dragon to find out why the two men have broken faith with her. (She's obviously been watching everything that's going on.) They don't get an answer and the trials continue.

(11) There's a scene in the garden where Pamina is resting and the chief slave, Monostatos, accosts her and tries to get her to marry him. He is a lecher. Then the Queen of the Night slips in and gives Pamina a dagger, telling her to murder Sarastro. The evil Monostatos overhears this and threatens her, but Sarastro, who is just behind him, saves her, explaining his philosophy of love. It's a rather funny bit, because immediately Monostatos says he's innocent, even after he's caught red-handed.

(12) In the next scene Papageno breaks his vow of silence and talks to an old hag who says she's his promised love and tells him he must swear to be true to her, or suffer serious penalties. When he swears to be faithful, she reveals herself as a young, beautiful girl. It's Papagena, but she's not quite ready for him, because he has not completed the journey, so she magically disappears. He is so sad that he's lost her that he decides to hang himself.

(13) The Three Ladies reappear and say, "Remember the magic bells we gave you?" As he plays the magic bells, Papagena comes out and there is a marvelous duet when they sing each other's names and speculate about all the little Papagenos and Papagenas they're going to have. There's a last effort by the Queen of the Night to take over the temple. She promises that if Monostatos helps her he can have Pamina in marriage, but the sublime light strikes them down as they try to get into the temple.

(14) Tamino and Pamina have now gone through the darkness and through the tests of fire and water, with the help of the magic flute, reaching a higher level of life, toward light. I interpret that as going towards the sun. Finally, Tamino and Pamina are joined in a grand wedding. Everybody is overjoyed that they have made the journey and they are taken into Sarastro's priestly order. At the end when the sun's rays strike out the darkness, all the players are brought together and everybody finds a partner. In that sense, it is about the union of all creatures, a universal theme.

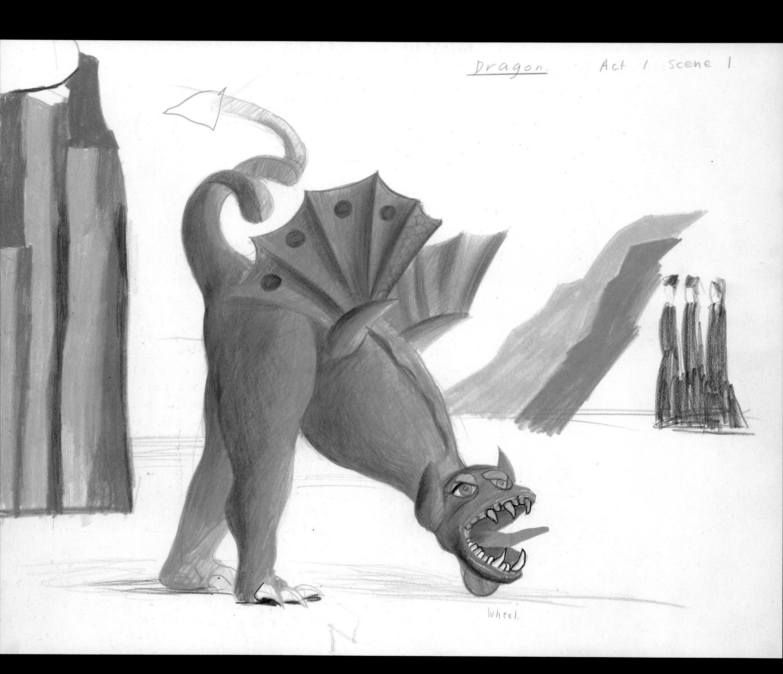

Dragon.   Act 1 scene 1

Wheel.

Designing
The Magic Flute

Martin Friedman and David Hockney

The Magic Flute has undergone seemingly endless interpretations since its 1791 premiere in Vienna. It has been played as a romantic comedy about the travails, separation and reunion of two sets of lovers, the aristocratic Tamino and Pamina and the earthy duo, Papageno and Papagena; it has been presented as a moralistic saga whose all too human principals must overcome innumerable physical and spiritual trials on the way to self-realization. There is sufficient ambiguity in its plot to allow for many readings, and under various directorial hands its comedic or spiritual qualities have at one time or another prevailed. Far more interesting than its youthful quartet are the characters of the Queen of the Night and the high priest Sarastro, the enigmatic personages who activate the physical and psychological terrain the foursome must traverse. Yet as Hockney points out, their roles are never precisely defined and *The Flute* remains an open-ended drama with constantly shifting meanings. The Queen and her Three Ladies, who rescue the hapless Tamino from the giant reptile, eventually turn out to be agents of darkness, determined to make things as difficult as possible for the wandering innocents. Her rival—or at least her opposite—is the benevolent Sarastro whom she falsely characterizes as an evil sorcerer. It is he, in fact, who presides over the harmonious domain where Wisdom, Reason and Nature flourish.

The Magic Flute, with text by Emanuel Schikaneder, the director of the Theater auf der Wieden, was, Hockney reminds us, written as popular entertainment, and Mozart wrote its music on commission. Since both were members of Freemason lodges, small coincidence that allusions to its practice exist in the opera, especially in the rituals over which Sarastro presides. Such references must have been relatively daring in late 18th-century Vienna where Freemasonry was incurring considerable hostility from the crown. Before starting to design *The Flute*, Hockney decided to learn as much as possible about its initial production at the Theater auf der Wieden. His research convinced him that Schikaneder's primary interest was to put something lively and amusing on stage that would please a large audience.

Dragon
drawing for *The Magic Flute* 1978
crayon on paper
14 × 17

Paolo Uccello
St. George and the Dragon   circa 1460
oil on canvas
22¼ × 29¼
Collection The National Gallery, London

Giotto
Flight into Egypt, Scrovegni Chapel, Padua   14th century
fresco

A lot has been written about Schikaneder's exploiting Mozart's talent—everybody runs him down. I'm just suggesting that he couldn't have been all bad, because if he had been, Mozart wouldn't have written such sublime music for him. I suspect he was probably a bit of a ham, wanting to hog the stage. I mean he played Papageno himself, didn't he? . . . It was as if David Merrick had asked Stravinsky to write something for Broadway. Stravinsky might have done it, whereas a lesser artist wouldn't have dared, because he wouldn't have the confidence that his art could rise above any vulgar ideas the plot might contain. Mozart must have taken such commissions often, and not just for the money. I don't believe he did anything for base reasons. There is certainly no sign of that in the work. Everything he did was treated seriously, even the comedies.

Whatever Schikaneder's motives in writing *The Magic Flute*, its ambiguity of plot has increased, if anything, over the past two-hundred years and its interpretation is still being debated. In fact, as Hockney admits, Glyndebourne's production, too, occasionally lacked clear focus, because he and the opera's director, John Cox, had somewhat divergent views in a few cases about what should take place on stage. As a result, both agree, its design problems were far greater than *The Rake*'s. Given the vague setting of the story, Hockney reflects, no single historical period could provide a comfortable format.

Although the libretto suggests it takes place in Old Kingdom Egypt, it doesn't really have to look like it. When I began doing research in the British Museum library I decided to look into the 18th-century European's view of Egypt and found it quite inventive. I found marvelous looking things, especially those that were completely wrong. For instance, many artists had made drawings of what they thought ancient Egypt looked like, and these were mostly based on descriptions of travelers. My designs for The Magic Flute *used that naive approach. They also reflect a Renaissance view of Egypt that you see in early Italian painting.*

In considering how he would design *The Flute*, Hockney opted for a lyrical fusion of exotic forms from all periods of history. The not-so-fierce scaly beast that assails Tamino was inspired by none other than the ornate, if unfortunate, dragon impaled on St. George's spear in Paolo Uccello's 15th-century Florentine masterpiece, a painting Hockney came to know in London's National Gallery during his student days. The more benign beasts of the forest, those improbable creatures charmed by the music of *The Flute*, came from medieval drawings of fantastic animals discovered while Hockney was browsing the British Museum's rare book room. The early Italian influences he discusses are the ingenuously painted landscapes found in the panel paintings of Giotto and his trecento contemporaries; such influence abounds in the near simplistic rendering of rocks, hills and trees in *The Flute*'s opening scene. A highpoint in Glyndebourne's production occurs when the huge Giottoesque boulder at center stage revolves and splits open to

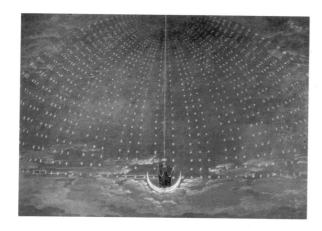

Karl Friedrich Schinkel
The Hall of Stars of the Queen of the Night stage design for *The Magic Flute*, Act 1, Scene 6   1816
gouache on paper
18½ × 24½
Collection Staatliche Museen, Berlin

The Metropolitan Museum of Art's grand interior staircase was the inspiration for Hockney's Great Hall in *The Magic Flute*.
1932 photograph

reveal the Queen of the Night in full voice. Hockney's research into earlier conceptions of this opera led him to the romantic visualizations of Karl Friedrich Schinkel, the eminent 19th-century German architect and scenic designer. In Schinkel's version, the Queen appears against a magnificent starry sky, and Hockney thought enough of that dazzling notion to design a variation on it.

His research also took him to the Metropolitan Museum of Art's enormous Egyptian collection, where he found a number of motifs that he integrated into his unusual scheme. The dominant feature, for example, of the elaborate room where Pamina is imprisoned by the evil slave Monostatos, is a pair of seated, jackal-headed deities facing one another. But his major discovery at the Metropolitan Museum, was its monumental staircase, which in transmuted version dominated *The Flute*'s great temple scene.

There are so many ways you can interpret The Magic Flute. *Even though John Cox and I had discussed many possibilities, once I got into the music, I tended to see things my own way. John had thought about Sarastro's kingdom as an ideal place, a utopia, but I saw it more geometrically. My concept was more abstract. It was a place of order and proportion and I expressed those ideas in straight lines. Here's one example. My set for the beginning of Act II is a symmetrical view of a palace garden that extends into deep space. The converging lines of palm trees and the pyramid in the distance give you that feeling. I suppose if I had directed it, Sarastro and his followers would have been placed formally within that framework to emphasize the set's perspective. But John actually wanted them seated in a circle on the floor, because his vision of Sarastro's kingdom was a kind of democracy. Mind you, he had a point. In the text, they take a vote to decide if they will allow Prince Tamino to enter the brotherhood. The horns sound, the drums beat, they raise their hands and say yes, they'll agree to it. John also wanted the priests to look like builders— workers. So when they first appear, they are carrying instruments: T-squares, rulers—things people building a city would have used. You see them in their shirtsleeves and aprons. When they're in the circle at the start of Act II, they are wearing blue robes. I thought they should have two costumes, so you would see both sides of them—as worker-priests.*

Once the visual style, however hybridized, had been established by Hockney, the next step was to use it to advance the action. Because Glyndebourne's small stage did not lend itself either to grand spectacle or complicated scene changes, he cast about for other means to provide dramatic changes of environment. His solution was to use as many illusionistically painted backdrops as possible to designate different locales. As with *The Rake*, he decided to work with models. The process began with a group of gouache paintings whose forms would be enlarged as background drops. Integral to his scheme were the distinctive cut-off corners of the Glyndebourne proscenium. In fact, he made a virtue of that architectural detail, using it as a point of departure in his designs. The coffered, beaded

The artist's 1977 photograph of Peter Schlesinger with the colossal statue of King Rameses II at Mit Rahineh (Memphis), near Cairo, Egypt, circa 1300 B. C.

Pyramid and Obelisks
model for *The Magic Flute*   1977
photographs on cardboard, tissue, wire
16¼ × 21¼ × 12¼

A Great Hall
model for *The Magic Flute*   1977
photographs on cardboard, tissue, wire
16¼ × 21¼ × 12¼

and otherwise ornamental ceilings in the opera's interior scenes echo the proscenium's strong shape. In addition to the large drops, Hockney designed several pairs of smaller set elements—mainly rocks, obelisks and classical columns—which, placed at either side of the stage in front of the backdrops, would serve as wings and heighten the spatial quality of each episode. He made large color photographs of each drop and wing element for the scale model of the Glyndebourne stage, and used these to work out the sequence of set changes.

Because Hockney thought the central theme of *The Magic Flute* was the progression from chaos to order, this idea governed his design. Thus, at the beginning of the opera, the Queen of the Night's kingdom appears as an untamed realm of unscalable mountains and desolate terrain. In contrast, Sarastro's harmonious domain is expressed in pure geometry. While working on *The Magic Flute*, Hockney continued to play its music on records and tapes and its purity, he felt, had to be echoed in his designs. This could best be done by eliminating all chiaroscuro ("No haze, not too many shadows," says Hockney). The result: images that are strong, unitary shapes in flat, almost poster-like style.

In Hockney's conception, *The Magic Flute* is a relatively fast-paced production that covers a fair amount of geography. Act I includes a mountainous landscape in the Queen's celestial realm, a polychromed room in Sarastro's palace, and the entrance to the high priest's domain marked by three small temples. In Act II we see a palm grove, the temple porch, the temple garden, the temple hall, a vault, and two spectacular phenomena: a great wall of fire and a gigantic waterfall through which Tamino and Pamina must pass. The opera's concluding moment is an epiphany—a bright yellow sun whose rays extend the length and breadth of the stage.

I've seen many Magic Flutes. *If it is performed in a fixed set you never get the sense of journey which is so important in Act II. It can even seem static, something we wanted to avoid. I tried to stay close to the text. When the libretto requires a big room, I decided, let's make it a great big room; if it says a garden, let's clearly make it a garden; if it says the vault of a temple, let's clearly make it look like one. By working in this way and emphasizing definite scene changes, you would understand that Tamino and Pamina were on a great symbolic journey. The idea was to show them always moving to some higher plane.*

Because of the physical and spiritual progression that characterizes *The Magic Flute*, he was forced to think about the production as a series of constantly changing situations, rather than as fixed tableaux. With intricate combinations of Glyndebourne's full and partial drops, operated like a row of window blinds, he could generate a rich profusion of imagery and make transitions from one scene to another seem effortless. One of the problems of having so many set changes was the time needed to accomplish these.

If you are going to do a lot of scenes for The Magic Flute, *you cannot have*

Painting the set for the interior of Sarastro's palace in *The Magic Flute*, at Glyndebourne Festival Opera, 1978.

A Room in Sarastro's Palace
model for *The Magic Flute* 1977
photographs on cardboard, tissue, wire
16 × 21¼ × 12¼

Grove with Three Temples
model for *The Magic Flute* 1977
photographs on cardboard, tissue, wire
16 × 21¼ × 12

even a two-minute interval between them. That's too long in the theater. If you have ten changes, that would be adding twenty minutes to the performance—which is certainly too much. You cannot do that.

Although, from a technical point of view he carried his theater design far beyond that of *The Rake*, there were some disappointments. For example, by the time he had worked out the intricate drop combinations for each scene he discovered there were no lines left in the fly gallery from which to lower the chariot carrying the Three Genies, whose job was to conduct Tamino to Sarastro's kingdom. The chariot, to his irritation, had to be rolled in from the wings.

However diverse their stylistic ancestry, *The Magic Flute* designs are remarkable for their compositional consistency. In these, Hockney moves back and forth with astonishing ease from one level of realism to another, from ingenious description to startling illusionism. The three small temples of Sarastro's kingdom and the giant rock from which the Queen of the Night emerges are the essence of simplicity; by contrast the fire and waterfall scenes and the temple staircase are astonishing trompe l'oeil events. Symmetry is the common demoninator in each scene. The pyramid, staircase and temple door are at the center of each stage picture. Whereas the sets for *The Rake's Progress* are distinguished by their overwhelming linear quality, *The Flute's* sets consist of large compartmentalized color masses.

Hockney, for all the inventiveness of his design, is essentially a traditionalist when it comes to setting the stage. He prefers the simple box set with side wings to, say, an artfully angled interior. To that end he has made fresh use of the conventional stage flat. He delights in the obvious artificiality of this ancient stage device, placing one painted flat behind another to suggest vast distance within Glyndebourne's small viewing box. He found another way to suggest infinite space. While making *The Flute* models he discovered that by cutting openings in the drops, he could achieve such an illusion. We see this superbly accomplished in the great staircase scene, in which large rectangular openings over the balustrade reveal a sky filled with rolling clouds. In reality, the sky backdrop is only a few feet behind the staircase drop, but the effect is of limitless distance.

Thanks to *The Magic Flute*, Hockney had to concern himself with the relationship of stage lighting to color. Though he had tested various lighting ideas on the models, he was far from certain about how these would work on stage.

During the lighting of The Rake's Progress, *I had kept quiet, because I knew so little about the process and the lighting man Robert Bryan was so good. That set was relatively simple to light, because it was done in a graphic style. Things were more complicated with* The Magic Flute. *When the Glyndebourne people who were going to work on it came to see the model in London, many questions were asked. "How would you do this? What material would you use for that?" And so on. We had a long session. I remember Robert Bryan's*

reaction. He said, "these flat sets will be very difficult to light." He was especially concerned because the theater hadn't used much painted scenery for a long time and most of what he had worked on was three-dimensional.

Now, lighting a three-dimensional set is easy, in a sense you can angle the light to model it with shadow. You can't do this with a flat, painted set. All you can do is put even light on it and change its color or intensity. It's no good moving a light to create an effect—it won't have an effect. Robert and I agreed to solve the problem together. Some scenes were easy, like the first one with the three-dimensional mountain. But when he worked on the waterfall scene, the lights flickered and danced at first. I sat in the theater and didn't say anything. Then he turned the work lights back on and sat there looking at the set. He turned to me and said, "It's better this way, isn't it?" I agreed. I realized what had happened. I had put the flickering effect in with paint and we didn't have to do it with light. The same thing happened when we tried to light the wall of fire that Tamino and Pamina walk behind. Those painted flames needed only a soft red glow. Because the scene lasts only two minutes, you can believe the fire. If you were to watch it for much longer, you wouldn't believe it, but for two minutes you go along with the magic and it's over. Then a big waterfall appears and you believe that for another two minutes.

Once Hockney and Robert Bryan had resolved the problem of evenly illuminating the flat sets, the tonality of each scene could be controlled. As a result it would now be possible for the audience to experience *The Flute*'s colors in all their clarity.

Everyone said the production was very colorful, though I did not think of it that way, because it was mostly the colors of the earth, mud and sand in Egypt: red, red ochre, yellow ochres. Even the blues were soft; they were Antwerp blues, not vivid cobalts or ultramarines.

The Magic Flute, which encouraged Hockney to think in terms of time and space, also led him to regard his new work as a form of environmental sculpture. But his painter's sensibility prevailed and the game of illusion was far more challenging to him than mere verisimilitude. It was more interesting to suggest endless space with fragile painted planes than to displace it with heavy volumes.

The closing scene of Act II from *The Magic Flute* as performed at Glyndebourne Festival Opera, 1978, in which Tamino and Tamina are wed and taken into Sarastro's order.

Hockney at the Met

John Dexter and Martin Friedman

When John Dexter proposed the French triple bill to the management of the Metropolitan, he regarded it as the culmination of the work he had set out to do as the company's director of production. His initial proposal contained everything he thought the Met should do to attract and dazzle its audience. Before Hockney's talents were enlisted, Dexter had visions of that evening at the Met as almost confrontational theater—with more than a whiff of Dada about it—in which the public would actually watch the production take form.

In a 5 July 1978 memo to the management, he suggested that this program, "if treated in the manner indicated in the synopsis, becomes not only a small exercise in the philosophy of theatrical mechanics, but an evening for us to really deploy all of our resources. In addition, it gives us an opportunity to turn the Met and the plaza into a gigantic musical amusement arcade. No one has to take every ride or play every game—the choice is up to them."

The original order of presentation suggested was *Les Mamelles de Tirésias*, *Parade* and *L'Enfant et les Sortilèges*. Before the audience arrives in the opera house, wrote Dexter, they will be

> . . . waylaid by Darius Milhaud on an improvised stage in the plaza. An Opera Studio group will be performing at about 7:30 pm–7:45 pm the first of Milhaud's Opéras-Minutes (eight minutes each opera, to be precise), time to end with sufficient interval for the audience to take their places in the auditorium where everything else seems to be normal. The comfortable gold curtain is down and the orchestra is in place in the pit. The chandeliers go away, the conductor comes out and we continue with all the normal flummery of an opera performance.

He goes on, describing his vision of the set for *Les Mamelles de Tirésias* whose stylistic ancestor, he says, might be René Clair's film, *The Italian Straw Hat*. During the first intermission he suggests the audience could either leave the theater or watch the scene change.

If the set change is not amusing enough, I would suggest that they are able to

Parade 1980
gouache, pencil, crayon on paper
22½ x 30
Private collection
Courtesy Andre Emmerich Gallery

turn to the second Milhaud opera which can be viewed either from the terrace or the plaza (if wet, in the garage area, Fire Department permitting). Should the open air not attract them, there will be on a podium on the Grand Tier level a pianist (backed by one of the Dufy cloths from C level) playing piano works of Ravel, Satie, Poulenc, etc. His position must be central and be capable of being listened to from all the foyer levels. (Dare I hope that for the opening gala this role will be played by Maestro James?) After this promenade they are then able to return to the theater for Parade.

Though Hockney's name was prominent in Dexter's proposal, the director continued his free-association process as to the appearance of the set for *Parade*. It should, he said, consist of:

one front cloth and one back cloth—either Picasso or Hockney pastiching Picasso. The whole ballet would be choreographed by Twyla Tharp and take place in front of one of these cloths. At the end of Parade *when the ballet have taken their last bows without use of the gold curtain, they divide at the middle, turn to the Picasso backdrop which flies away to reveal the stage crew who proceed to make the second intermission features.*

In this case, Hockney agreed with Dexter about doing a variation on Picasso's painted curtain, with its winged horse and acrobats. For the second intermission feature preceding *L'Enfant*, Dexter suggests that the pianist in the foyer play one of Milhaud's *Opéras-Minutes* to gain the audience's attention. Those remaining in the auditorium could watch the elevation of the orchestra pit and the soloists and children's chorus taking their places. *L'Enfant*, he says, should

be sung, mimed and played out front and ought to represent a climax in the evening of a clear statement of a theatrical philosophy that true magic can only exist in theater when you show quite clearly you have nothing up your sleeve.

Dexter's first concept for *L'Enfant* was to have the soloists rise and sing. The part of the wicked little boy would be mimed in ordinary clothes. He proposed that various members of the chorus carry emblems or masks representing animals in the garden: dragonflies, bats, frogs and other characters.

While carrying the emblem or mask, their bodies must move as they think the element or animal would move and so the visual picture will be standing on the raised orchestra pit in everyday clothes, acting out with masks. At the end of the evening, order will be restored by the lowering of the comfortable gold curtain, and the audience, as they leave, may stop to be entertained by a combo (American) playing jazz of the period 1900–30 in the plaza, so that the absent composers may pay a debt and the audience be reminded of the American contribution to the evening.

Once Dexter began working with Hockney, the street theater aspects of his initial scheme disappeared. There was another reason for modifying his idea: evidently, the management did not share his enthusiasm for the ancillary performances he wanted to occur outside the Met itself. Thus, the carnival-like events in the plaza did not take place, nor did a pianist offer Milhaud and jazz between the acts. But if the evening turned out to be less free-form than he had anticipated, it took on other qualities: intense lyricism and rich fantasy. His interaction with Hockney provided a seemingly endless sequence of episodes in which music, costumes and set elements were vividly interrelated. There was no shortage of invention on the stage.

Dexter's arrival at the Metropolitan in 1974 as director of production followed a successful career in England. He was an actor in the Derby Repertory Company, along with such notable contemporaries as Alan Bates and John Osborne. During the run of Osborne's *Look Back in Anger* at the Royal Court Theatre, Dexter assumed the duties of assistant director. In 1963 he was invited by Laurence Olivier to the National Theatre, where he directed *Saint Joan, Othello, The Misanthrope, Equus, The Life of Galileo, The Shoemaker's Holiday* and many other productions. Having established himself as a director, he took on additional assignments in London's West End and on New York's Broadway.

Dexter's first experience with opera was the 1966 Convent Garden revival of Berlioz's *Benvenuto Cellini* and, through a chance meeting with Rolf Liebermann at the Hamburg State Opera, he was invited to direct a number of productions there, including *Un Ballo in Maschera, Boris Godounov, Billy Budd* and *From the House of the Dead*. His first project for the Metropolitan was *I Vespri Siciliani* in 1974.

Since I came to the Met, I have been very conscious that someone had to do something about making 20th-century works acceptable to the Metropolitan audience. Both James Levine and I were agreed that we needed to present works by Berg, Stravinsky and other important composers. The question was how to go about it. I came up with an economic solution: sell it to them through Dialogues des Carmélites, *a 20th-century piece that was not too costly to produce. It did work—it did 95–98 percent business.*

While doing Carmélites, *I had the idea for a triple bill, which is supposed to be death in an opera house. To me, these three 20th-century French works had always seemed related: Satie's* Parade, *Poulenc's* Les Mamelles de Tirésias *and Ravel's* L'Enfant et les Sortilèges. *One of the relationships, apart from the purely nationalistic one, was they were all conceived during the First World War when the Germans were about thirty miles from Paris. They all sprang out of French culture at a time when it was under the greatest possible threat. The three composers and Apollinaire, made deeply aware by the First World War of the mentality of war, the waste of it, the mindlessness of it, attacked it with irony and tenderness.*

Apollinaire arrived wounded from the front to attend the premiere of Parade *in 1917, so for our production it seemed there was a poetic point to be made by using barbed wire on the stage to suggest that war is always imminent. Don't forget the theme he presents in the scenario of* Les Mamelles: *"We need more*

babies, make more babies." It doesn't come through in performance unless you are French and for people who are not, the barbed wire serves to remind them of when, how and why the French government was ordering people to have larger families. The possibility of war surrounds us all the time and particularly threatens the lives of our children. By using a child and a harlequin at the beginning of Parade and at the end of L'Enfant, I hoped to make the point that the only sanity for our children is in the arts—music, painting, literature. The only thing that any civilization is remembered by is its art and we'd better, I think, consider that when we come to educating our children.

After I had gone through the battle of getting the idea for the French triple bill at the Met accepted, I asked David Hockney to design it. I'd met him once, briefly, at the Royal Court when he was doing Ubu Roi and had seen all his work from the very beginning, because I used to putter around the galleries. I had seen The Rake, which was very good, and Flute, which was very good, but Ubu Roi had some of the madness I was looking for—so many parts of it had so much, especially the Polish army scene. His work also had the sense of movement and color I thought could translate directly to theater. But we'd never really met although we come from within thirty miles of each other in England and everyone used to say we had a lot in common.

The French triple bill was such a delicate operation that I wasn't in a mood to take chances with its design. I thought about it very carefully, but not for long, because David was in it from the beginning without his knowing it. I wrote him a fairly detailed letter outlining my idea for the evening, letting him know why I wanted to work with him and that it would not be all that easy. When I went to Los Angeles to talk to him about it, he grabbed at the idea and started working immediately on a number of approaches to the three events.

Dexter's letter to Hockney (25 September 1978) detailed a strong scheme to create a total theatrical evening from three heretofore unrelated works. He also stated his intention to have the Metropolitan Opera present important contemporary works and develop new audiences for these. The triple bill would be the first step of Dexter's three-year plan. His letter expressed the hope that Parade, as the entire evening came to be called, would initiate and ". . . celebrate this jump into another area of the opera house with a parade of all the things which have never normally been permitted in that august establishment."

Dexter had already spoken with Rudolf Nureyev about doing the choreography for Parade and in recruiting Hockney believed he was assembling a strong artistic unit whose members would interact creatively. It soon became clear, however, that Nureyev had an extremely different view of Parade, one at odds with Dexter's conception of its role in the triple bill. Nureyev wanted to do a ballet about the meeting of Satie, Picasso, Cocteau and Diaghilev, the creators of the original Parade. However, artistic differences led to Nureyev's withdrawal from the project, to be replaced by Gray Veredon.

Curtain with Square Stage and Floorboards
drawing for Les Mamelles de Tirésias   1980
crayon on paper
18¾ × 24
Private collection, courtesy Andrew Crispo Gallery

Dexter's convictions about what constitutes theatrical experience have taken him into areas other than "directing traffic on the stage." Shortly after his arrival, his interest in the visual aspects of theater became apparent to Met audiences in his starkly elegant productions of *Dialogues des Carmélites* and *Billy Budd.*

When David came to look over the Met space, we agreed that something had to be done to relate the vast stage to the audience. I've always had strong feelings about how the space could be used to intensify the dramatic and visual qualities of our productions. When I first arrived there, I found they were only really using three quarters of their proscenium height. Those great gold drapes were always chopping it off and the further back in the house you went, the more it was like looking into a letterbox opening. The proscenium size you actually saw in no way related to the volume of the house itself. You couldn't let the audience feel you were shutting them off from the vital action on the stage. So, beginning with Carmélites *and carrying on through* Billy Budd, *I removed the gold valance and used the proscenium's full height. Now you could sit at the very back of the family circle and feel you were seeing the whole space of the stage.*

David and I didn't have to discuss the issue of opening the stage. He knew right away what I wanted. His approach was to study the house from all possible angles. Indeed, most designers working in a new house do that automatically. They will look at the stage from all the awkward viewing positions, not just the far away ones, and make notes. I said to David, "You know, one of the biggest problems you're going to have is the actual look of the house itself. We have to find ways of breaking into that." Once David had mastered the geography of the Met, we began collaborating on the production designs in earnest.

Originally, the idea was to have Parade *in the middle, not as a prelude. But after about six months it seemed to me that the best thing would be to treat it exactly as the French would have, not as Cocteau's ballet with its complicated little episodes, but as a simple parade before a performance introducing all the elements that were going to appear throughout the evening—not only the characters of the child and harlequin, but also the visual elements that would help tie the production together—the alphabet blocks, the ladder and circus ball. Our idea was that this motley group of acrobats, magicians, dancers and other circus types would perform in front of a painted curtain behind which the audience would be led to believe the major theatrical event would occur.*

In devising his scheme for *Parade,* Dexter acknowledges the help of composer Henri Sauguet, a friend of the original *Les Six,* and of the Cocteau estate. From these sources he had access to letters, photographs and information on Satie's ideas for *Parade.* He also referred to Cocteau's rehearsal drawings and diaries describing the preparation of the original production in 1917.

Though Parade *was the last of the three Met works to be designed, we*

Dancers from Nijinsky's 1913 *Sacre du Printemps* with costumes by Nicholas Roerich. (This is the only known image of these costumes. In it, the figures were cut out and superimposed on the Roerich backdrop.)

Costumes for the 1920 *Sacre du Printemps*, choreographed by Leonide Massine. These and Roerich's 1913 version were closely related models for the Hockney/Dexter production.

decided to open the evening with it. It's a germinal piece of music that can be interpreted time and again. I realize that people get sentimental about the original Massine/Picasso collaboration, but when Massine was reviving it for the Joffrey in 1973, he told the dancer Gary Chryst that the new production was not a pure reconstruction. In fact, he told Chryst it bore little resemblance to the original, because he could scarcely remember it. So, people were really being nostalgic about something they saw at the Joffrey a few years ago, not that night in 1917 when it was first performed at the Théâtre du Châtelet.

As Dexter's conception of the *Parade* evening evolved, he was in touch with the venerable French conductor, Manuel Rosenthal, celebrated for his interpretations of the music of Ravel, his one-time mentor. Rosenthal's ideas about early 20th-century French music, his friendship with its Parisian creators, made him a natural choice to conduct the three French works. In a 29 April 1980 letter to Rosenthal, Dexter expressed his feelings about bringing together this trio of French modernist works. In it he agrees with the critic Richard Buckle who referred to Satie's *Parade* as the doorway to the 20th-century theater. In the letter, Dexter also invokes the spirit of Guillaume Apollinaire, the visionary who called for the creation of such new theater. In fact, the Metropolitan's program for the French triple bill contained Apollinaire's statement, which had appeared in the preface to his 1903 play *Les Mamelles de Tirésias* and which, Dexter says, continues to guide his thinking:

One tries here to infuse a new spirit to the theatre,
A joy, a delight, a virtue,
To replace this pessimism, more than a century old,
Which is quite ancient for such a boring thing.
The play was written for an ancient stage
Because one wouldn't have built a new theatre for us,
A round theatre with two stages,
One in the center, the other one like a ring
Round the audience and which would permit the expression of
The big display of our modern art.
Putting together often without any visible link, as in life,
The sounds, the gestures, the colors, the cries, the noises,
The music, the dance, the acrobaticism, the poetry, the painting,
The chorus, the actions, and the multiple decors.

I wanted the evening to make several points, not only about the salvation of humanity through art, but also about a new kind of theater that could change the relationship of the audience to the actor. Consequently, that statement by Apollinaire was important to the conception of the French triple bill and, later, to the Stravinsky evening. Indeed, it remains important to all my work because by bringing together opera, ballet, drama and painting, I hoped to produce a strong, unified statement. Opera audiences no longer go to ballet; ballet audiences no longer go to opera; a few of each go to the theater. They need to be reunited rather forcefully and that's really what I wanted to initiate at the Metropolitan Opera over the next few years.

David and I met again in another couple of months in Los Angeles to talk about the structure of the triple bill and to discuss specifics. He had produced half a dozen different versions of the Normandy house and garden for the Ravel. That was also when he came up with the idea of using huge alphabet blocks as a visual theme to help relate the three French operas. We agreed that the scenery, in addition to its color, feel and intensity, must have a dynamic of movement about it; otherwise, you're lost. That's why I responded to the blocks he left around. We decided on how many we would need to spell Maurice Ravel, then decided to carry the motif through the whole evening, also spelling Satie's and Poulenc's names. Thus the blocks became a device that would begin the evening and that people would still find acceptable by the time we got to L'Enfant. I then suggested it might be interesting to use the other sides of the blocks to make up the furniture—the armchair, fireplace and other objects in the room—and he said, well, it would take a bit of working out. So we sat and worked it out. Serendipity, is that the word? That's the way we work together.

For Les Mamelles de Tirésias David first proposed a rather elaborate, nearly cubistic set for the mythical town of Zanzibar in southern France. That was one of the earliest versions. Not disagreeing with him, I said, "Well, look, I wanted a very simple pastiche of an Edwardian musical comedy—three sets made of cut cloth surrounded by the darker space of war."

Hockney began designing Les Mamelles and L'Enfant in Los Angeles and in 1980, while Dexter was in London directing The Life of Galileo at the National Theatre, he worked on these designs in his London studio.

We arrived at a working method. Realizing the difficulties of developing a design from sketches, I said you must work from a model. You can have a quarter-inch model. He said, "I can't work at a quarter inch, it's too small." So I had a big one made. It was really the only way I could think of to get him to deal with specifics. Sometimes he can be exasperating. I've worked with Laurence Olivier for fifteen or twenty years; for two weeks during rehearsals of Othello, Larry disappeared from the world; you couldn't contact him at all. He was working out his own problems, which he had to do. But when you didn't know that was happening, it was very difficult. I learned that he would eventually come back and to give him time, and what I learned on Olivier I used on Hockney! Whenever he goes off into an area which is absolutely irrelevant or repeats himself for the one hundred ninety-ninth time and goes on with the same point, you just say, "Yes, David, yes." I also just sort of say Othello! Othello! Othello! and let him go on until he's talked himself out. I wait for a moment until I'm sure, and say yes, that's what we agreed on two days ago. Now we can get back to work. He would show me a model of a set and I'd say, can you cut a bit off that or take a bit off this? He allowed me to do

Punchinellos Changing Blocks
drawing for *Parade* evening   1980
gouache on paper
14 × 17

that. If he hadn't, I don't know if we could have worked together. But he did, and we do, and that's that.

As the action shifted to the Metropolitan stage, Hockney familiarized himself with the great range of facilities: scene shops, wardrobe, and the other incomparable resources that make up the Met's technical departments. Though his painted designs were faithfully enlarged, constant modifications were required to achieve the desired visual and dramatic effects. This meant that considerable improvisation was necessary. For example, the giant alphabet blocks that were to spell the composers' names had to be designed for easy manipulation by the children.

Dealing with human scale has been the problem from the beginning at the Met and that question was basic to L'Enfant. We used children, dressed as little punchinellos, to move the exaggerated furniture about, making it look all the larger in the child's dream. I used the children's chorus because most of them have some musical instinct and are used to being on stage without being show-biz kids. We had a couple of those and got rid of them. The first and most difficult problem David had to decide on was the right height for an alphabet block that a child could carry. A row of blocks had to read as Maurice Ravel and a pile of them had to look like a piece of furniture from the back of the auditorium.

The rehearsal blocks were made of lightweight composition board and had come down from the prop shop with vague markings on them. What the prop shop hadn't understood was that the children would be able to see them only from the back, so the back of each block had to be marked as clearly as the front as to the element it represented. This wasn't done and there was considerable confusion in rehearsal. David came to the rescue and we spent a lot of time that afternoon with the kids splashing paint on the blocks to make clear their specific meanings.

Moving the blocks about had been worked out on the model, but working it out with kids of twelve, thirteen and fourteen was a different matter. You've got the questions of size and weight; are their arms long enough to lift them? Have you miscalculated anything? You have to let them find their way around it. You explain it to them, you explain they are punchinellos and are invisible, technically. Their costumes will make them invisible. David's being there certainly helped.

Though critical and popular response to the French triple bill was decidedly positive—and the box office reflected this, too—Dexter, after the initial performance, wanted to make a number of changes in staging that would strengthen his idea that the three works were strongly related and shared common themes. Through a child's eyes we can experience the wondrous effects of all the arts and, on a darker level, the child's life is in mortal danger so long as war is a constant threat. So individualistic and self-contained were these works that even with the theatrical device of the child and his harlequin guide moving from one production to the other, Dexter felt his message was

Child with Large Chair and Fireplace
drawing for *L'Enfant et les Sortilèges* 1980
gouache on paper
14 × 17

134

not as clear as it should be. To ensure a greater sense of totality, he proposed a number of changes for the 1982 revival of the French triple bill.

In Parade *I plan to trim the ballet and keep things simple. There would be no silly people rushing about and going into the circus tent to see the show. I would make no attempt to go near the complicated Cocteau scenario with all the subplots of acrobats, managers and magicians doing separate things. There was too much concentration on the relationships among the figure of war, the child and the harlequin. I want a simple parade in which all the lions, tigers, clowns and punchinellos appear briefly, thus announcing the sort of evening it's going to be. That's what a parade is. Cocteau wanted one kind of parade; we, with Apollinaire, saw another kind emerging from these three musical events.*

Our original idea for L'Enfant *was that at the end of the garden scene the animals would begin to fight viciously among themselves and slowly, the garden would disappear. You would be left with blackness and barbed wire. In the revival, I still hope to get the final image I wanted: a return to the barbed wire so the child's cry for Maman when all this happens in the garden is more a warning to the audience.*

Indeed, in the 1982 revival, Dexter made most of these changes, and though it meant that some of Hockney's costumes for the ballet were eliminated, the evening gained in clarity.

During a final technical rehearsal for *Parade*, Dexter decided to ask Hockney to collaborate with him on another triple bill, three Stravinsky works: *Le Sacre du Printemps, Le Rossignol* and *Oedipus Rex.* He had originally begun working on it with Jocelyn Herbert who soon left the project as she was unable to leave England at that time. As a result, the usual lead time was not available to Hockney and the production had to be realized within twelve months. The sessions began at Dexter's house in Atlantic Highlands, New Jersey, where the pair rapidly decided on such fundamentals as circles and masks as unifying motifs. Shortly afterward, Hockney sent the director sketches for the Chinese emperor's palace in *Rossignol* and for the *Oedipus* set. Both drawings stressed the tiers curving around the Met auditorium and indeed these were incorporated in the design. Scrawled on the drawing was Hockney's note asking if Dexter thought the circular schemes might work.

Dexter and Hockney were determined that the Stravinsky triple bill should offer a strong contrast to the French evening which, for all its anti-war sentiment, was perceived by the audience as a warm and lyrical event. Aside from the fact that the works in the triple bill were by the same composer, commonalities had to be stressed through direction and production design. This would be an evening of ritual. The primitivism of *Sacre*, the artificial refinement of *Rossignol*'s Chinese court, the preordained fate of Sophocles's doomed king lent themselves to this concept.

The Stravinsky evening had to be more contained than the French one. It was an occasion for our saying to ourselves over and over again, "less, less, less."

Stravinsky Triple Bill, Study for Curtain 1981
crayon and gouache on paper
14 × 17

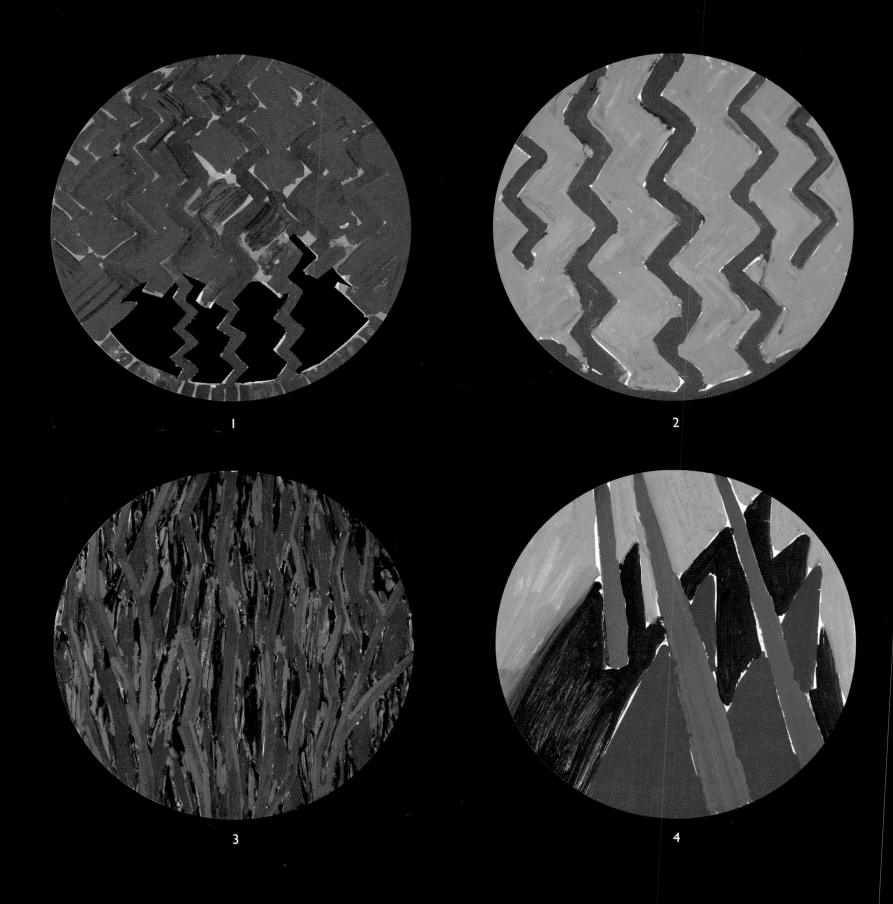

1

2

3

4

We were making our homage to the circle and the mask—all kinds of masks and all kinds of circles. After all, theater began in a circle with somebody telling a story around a fire.

It was Stravinsky's music that gave the evening its unity. You sensed these weren't three Stravinsky stage works, it was one Stravinsky evening and the works related to one another. The intellectual, emotional and musical strength you feel coming from Stravinsky was the first thing we tried to express visually and the circle was the natural basic form. Listening to his music, you're aware of the danger, you're aware of the risk and you're aware of his perpetual challenge to the audience. He once said to Manuel Rosenthal, "We have the right to do everything except bore audiences." Absolutely perfect! I love listening to Stravinsky because of the tension, because of the challenge, because of the excitement, because of the demands it makes on me. It forces your attention, forces you to change your perceptions of what listening is.

Once again, Dexter and Hockney had to leave the design of a ballet until last. Though the circle motif had been decided upon, there was another basic question in *Sacre* to be settled. Where does it take place? Unlike *Rossignol* and *Oedipus* which suggest specific locales—an emperor's palace and Thebes—the ballet has usually been perceived as occurring in the murky realm of generalized primitivism. *Sacre*, of course, has long been a favorite of ballet companies, largely because its sacrifice-of-the-virgin theme and violent percussive rhythms could justify the wildest gymnastics, performed under conditions of near nudity. In the publication, *Stravinsky in Pictures and Documents*, by Vera Stravinsky and Robert Craft, *Sacre du Printemps* is described as a musical-choreographic work that "represents pagan Russia and is unified by a single idea: the mystery and great surge of the creative power of spring." The Dexter/Hockney version coincides with Stravinsky's idea of locating it in a cold, stark setting.

There have been many Sacres which you think are taking place in high summer; so many beautiful naked bodies fluttering all over the stage. Originally, we also went much too "hot" with it; I had a book on face painting that Teresa Stratas had given me, called The People of Kau, *by Leni Riefenstahl. The faces were black-and-white and brown-and-white and really heavily textured. We began with that idea, then drifted away because David thought it was too hot, though oddly enough, we ended up with very severe, painted faces, not unlike those photographed by Riefenstahl.*

Though David made a great number of sketches for the costumes, on stage at the first rehearsal they seemed too elegant. The choreographer Jean-Pierre Bonnefous sat with us and he, David and I agreed they had to be changed. They had to become heavier. We felt we had to break into that rather beautiful classical line with coarse, heavy material. The costumes didn't look primitive enough. Too sophisticated. David and Jean-Pierre went up to wardrobe, chose some other material, and made three or four new costumes—much heavier looking. We liked them and said, "Right, go ahead and do the whole lot!" (This

1 *Sacre du Printemps, Sacre Disc I*   1981
gouache on cardboard
16½ d

2 *Sacre du Printemps, Sacre Disc II*   1981
gouache on cardboard
16½ d

3 *Sacre du Printemps, Sacre Disc VII*   1981
gouache on cardboard
12 d

4 *Sacre du Printemps, Sacre Disc XV*   1981
gouache on cardboard
12 d

These detail photographs of Chinese blue-and white porcelain were taken by the artist in London's Victoria and Albert Museum as a part of his research for the design of Stravinsky's *Le Rossignol*.

Sacre du Printemps, Dancers Pushing Hands   1981
gouache on paper
22½ × 30

put something of a strain on the budget, but we were still under budget at the end of the whole thing, so we lost a little of what we'd saved—but it was worth it.) Remember, we wanted our production to be a bleak, Russian spring. Freezing cold. Between every bar of music, the ice is breaking.

When the curtain fell on *Sacre*, there was no effort to provide a transition to the next work other than through the front curtain painted with a huge circle composed of green, blue and red segments. Although the intention was to stress the ritualistic relationship among these works, the transitions between each were abrupt and the change of mood from the feverishness of *Sacre* to the coolness of *Rossignol* could not have been more drastic. Utterly devoid of threat or violence, *Rossignol* materialized in a delicate haze of color and sound.

The final design for *Rossignol* varied little from Hockney's first proposals. While he says the inspiration was 18th-century blue-and-white porcelain that he had encountered in the Chinese section of the Victoria and Albert Museum, Dexter has a slightly different account.

David came up to visit me in Derbyshire. I was in a hotel near to Chatsworth House. Well, Chatsworth had an enormous amount of porcelain, so we wandered around under the eye of God knows how many curators photographing stuff there. The emperor's palace was there and so was the special opalescent quality of the porcelain glaze. In fact, the theme of Rossignol *was already blue and white for me even before David went off to the V and A to photograph that collection.*

Rossignol *is a fairy story. It's neither a dream nor a fantasy. It is a way of telling a moral tale to children. The fisherman and the servant girl are the only two who recognize the absolute voice of beauty when they hear it. The rest do not. In the dance it was our intention that the fisherman, danced by Anthony Dowell, be the partner of the nightingale who would be danced by Natalia Makarova. In fact, one of the earliest notes I sent our choreographer, Frederick Ashton, was that the fisherman was available for partnering—mainly because I know Sir Fred's delight in complicated lifts. Also, if you want to give an impression of a bird moving through the air, you lift.*

Once *Oedipus* had been selected, Dexter began studying the Cocteau text, carefully. Stravinsky required the soloists and chorus to sing in Latin, but he felt that the narrator should speak in the language of the country in which the opera-oratorio would be performed.

I got crosser and crosser with the e.e. cummings translation of the narrator's part, so I had to re-translate all the French. I realized that cummings's version was brilliant, but it didn't speak in the way that Cocteau speaks in French, which is harsh, distant, non-musical. I think it lost a bit of the purpose, so I sat down and got my schoolboy French to work and re-translated lines. I played the Cocteau recording until I got his rhythms and vowel sounds into my head and then tried it again.

Oedipus Rex was in strong contrast to the silken *Rossignol* that preceded it.

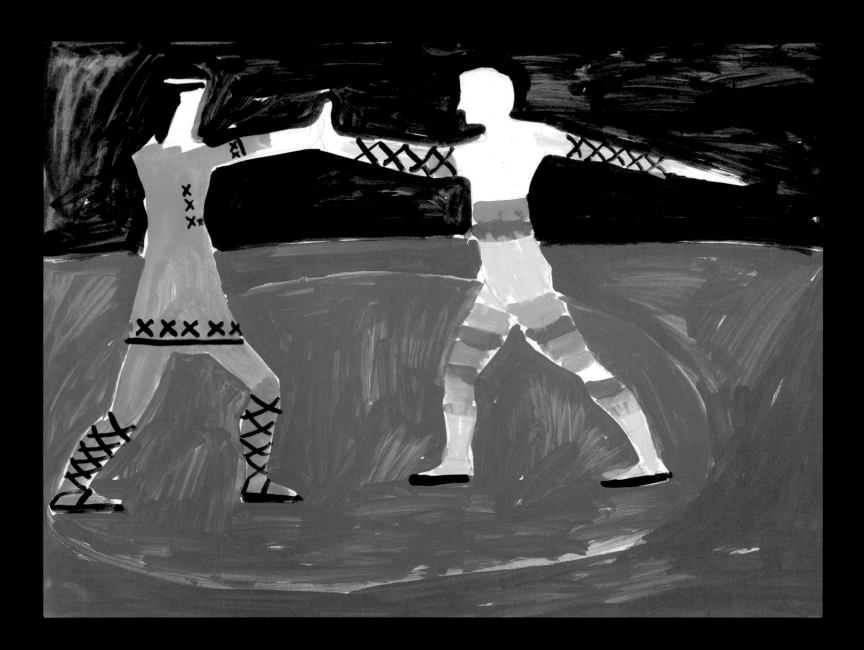

Oedipus Rex, Study for Masks II 1981
gouache on paper
23 × 29

Oedipus Rex, Principal Singers and Chorus 1981
gouache and tempera on paper
23 × 29

140

Again, the great scrim on which was emblazoned a monumental red, blue and green circle was raised to reveal a stage that seemed enormous, even by Met standards. Unlike the turbulence of *Sacre* or the fragile lyricism of *Rossignol*, the quality of *Oedipus* was at once ominous and riveting. Its protagonists were frozen beings, with only a few hieratic gestures made by the principals: Oedipus, his mother Jocasta, her brother-in-law Creon and the blind seer, Tiresias.

Attired in tuxedos, the chorus of sixty singers, seated in a line across the stage, close to the audience, formed a strong black and white unit with the similarly-clad orchestra below. On a red dais were the protagonists of Sophocles's drama. Seated on a throne-like chair at the orchestra level was the English dancer Anthony Dowell who spoke the fateful lines.

On the dais, four attendants held huge white helmet-like masks over the seated soloists and as each performer rose to sing a mask covered his or her face.

Oedipus was difficult to teach the singers; to give them the confidence to do nothing except one gesture, but in intellectual terms, it was the easiest to achieve. It arrived that first weekend and that's how it stayed.

The working relationship between Dexter and Hockney evolved to the point where each felt challenged, indeed pushed, by the other. Dexter more than realized the goal he posited in his initial letter to Hockney: they did engage in a "creative collision." His gamble was more than justified.

I once muttered to him, "David, this is the perfect chance for one of your portraits, because the only way you're going to get me is if you have me talking to you, so you'd better put a mirror on the wall and paint yourself into the conversation."

When he invited me to sit for him, I said it would be a pleasure, and let's find the time. We did find a date: it was Macy's Thanksgiving Day Parade. I went around to his studio for a couple of hours and he started working, but we left soon afterward to watch the fun. I think we will get around to it again soon, but it will probably take another collaboration, or another Macy's parade.

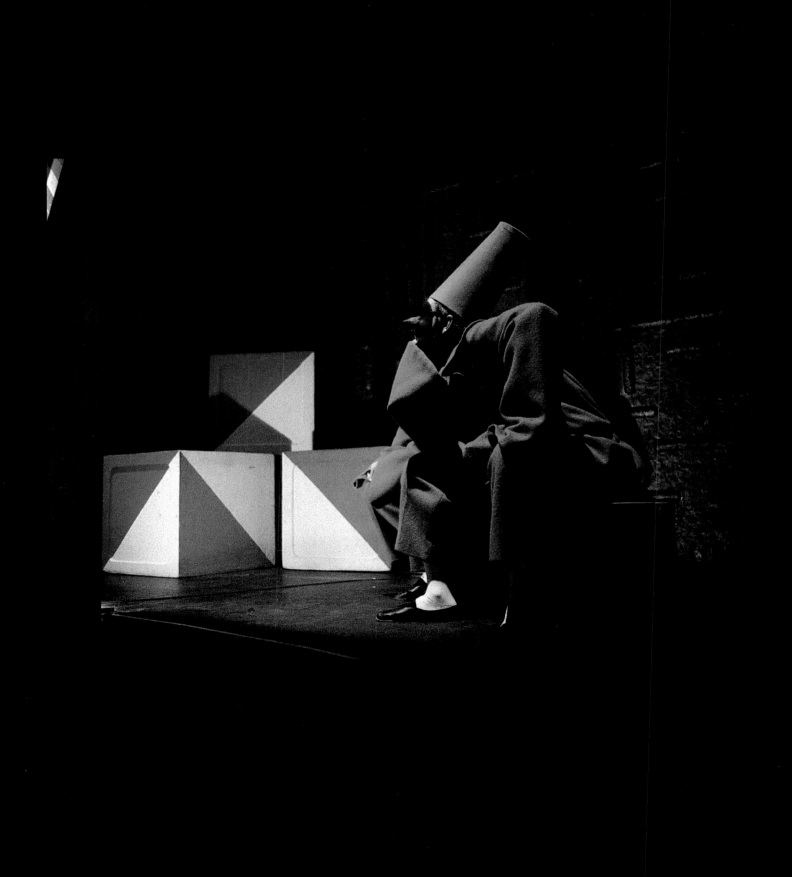

Parade

as told by David Hockney

Production series from *Parade,* as performed at the
Metropolitan Opera House, December, 1982. (See
Opera Chart, p 217) Harlequin: Gary Chryst, Columbine:
Antoinette Peloso, Chinese Conjuror: Roberto Medina

*(1) Satie's Parade does not have much of a story, so we used the ballet as a way
to introduce the characters who appear as the triple bill progresses.*

*(2) The evening opens with a group of soldiers moving across a battlefield. Barbed
wire, searchlights and a French flag make up this rather grim scene. But one of
the soldiers removes his gas mask and uniform to reveal himself as a harlequin.*

(3) He is the guardian spirit of a little boy whom he leads from the fury of war to safety. At one point he drives off a soldier who is attempting to hand this child a gun. Instead of the gun the harlequin offers puppets of himself and Columbine.

(4) When the harlequin and the child leave the circle of barbed wire, the harlequin looks up and pulls down a red curtain. Some of the characters in soldier costumes bring alphabet blocks onto the stage and line them up to spell "Erik Satie."

(5) The harlequin then seats the little boy on the prompter's box from where he will observe everything. Then the harlequin returns to the center of the stage and with various gestures introduces the evening's cast of characters. Some will appear only in the Satie ballet, such as Columbine, the Chinese Conjuror and the Stage Manager. Their costumes are direct quotes from Picasso's 1917 designs.

(6) Other characters who are in the Poulenc and Ravel works come on stage. They include Thérèse, from Les Mamelles and the cats from L'Enfant et les Sortilèges. As the ballet ends, the blocks are arranged in front of a blue fleur-de-lis curtain. This time they spell the words "Francis Poulenc," to prepare the audience for Les Mamelles, the opera to follow.

Les Mamelles de Tirésias

as told by David Hockney

Production series from *Les Mamelles de Tirésias*, as performed at the Metropolitan Opera House, December, 1982. (See Opera Chart, p 217) Thérèse: Catherine Malfitano, Gendarme: John Darrenkamp, Husband: David Holloway.

(1) It's a mad plot, a plotless play, that takes place in Zanzibar, an imaginary town in France, somewhere, perhaps, between Nice and Monte Carlo. The set looks like a typical little Mediterranean port town. The main characters are Thérèse and the husband. Thérèse is fed up with being a woman—she thinks it's all drudgery, too much housework, too many babies.

(2) She wishes to be something else, and so she ties up her poor husband and tells him they're going to exchange roles and he can take care of having children. It happens: her breasts (red and blue balloons) fly away and suddenly she has a beard. She and her husband change sexes and she becomes Tirésias, a man, and leaves home.

(3) Two drunks, Lacouf and Presto, appear. One says, we're in Zanzibar and the other says, no, we're in Paris. They argue and finally have a duel. They pull their guns at the same time and shoot each other dead. A chorus sings about the death of Lacouf and Presto—they think it's all a shame. A gendarme makes an entrance and falls in love with the husband who is now dressed in Thérèse's dress, but when he tries to make love to him, the husband puts him off and he departs. Lacouf and Presto enter again; they have come back to life, rolling in on scooters. Everybody sings.

(4) Then there's a small intermezzo between the acts: a gavotte, a little dance. By the time you open up on Act II, the husband has already given birth to more than forty thousand children, some of whom he's nursing. Some are in a row of perambulators at the front of the stage. A reporter comes in to interview the husband, thinking that the father of so many children must be a very rich man. One of the children has already written a best-selling novel, and the husband gives it to the reporter to read. After some unfavorable comments about it the journalist finally asks him for a loan and is politely thrown out.

(5) The husband then decides he can make more children by using the cubist idea of collage. He rips up a newspaper, puts it in a pram, puts in some glue and lo and behold, he makes a journalist! But the child is a disappointment to his dad, for he attempts to blackmail him. And, like the first reporter, he is gently sent away.

(6) Finally, Tirésias (Thérèse) enters disguised as a fortune-teller. After a bit of soothsaying, she reveals herself as a woman to her husband and they come around to the fact that they'd both be better off as they were, a proper man and woman. The sex changes are reversed. They are again man and wife and the point is, make babies, not war.

L'Enfant
et les Sortilèges

as told by David Hockney

Production series from L'Enfant et les Sortilèges, as performed at the Metropolitan Opera House, December, 1982. (See Opera Chart, p 217) Child: Hilda Harris, Mama: Isola Jones, Princess: Gail Robinson, Mr. Arithmetic: Joseph Frank, Fire: Myra Merritt, Grandfather Clock: David Holloway, Squirrel: Florence Quivar, Dragonfly: Ariel Bybee.

(1) L'Enfant is about a little boy who has no name; the setting is a farmhouse in Normandy. Colette wrote the story around 1917—that's the period in which the opera occurs. I've been to Normandy and I know those farmhouses. She describes the house as having a very low ceiling with beams and a large fireplace.

(2) As the music begins, you imagine the fire making dancing shadows in the room, and these are mysterious to the child. Anyway, the mother comes into the room. You don't actually see her; you see her huge shadow on the wall.

(3) She tells the child that until he's done all his homework and been a good boy he may have only dry bread and tea without sugar. She leaves a tray with a black Wedgewood teapot and a china cup on it and says, "Now, baby"—she calls him a baby—"be a good boy!" When she leaves, the little boy says he's fed up with being good—"I want to be free and wicked, wicked, wicked!"

(4) He rushes over and smashes the teapot, he breaks the cup, he jabs the squirrel with his pen, he pulls the tail of the cat sitting by the fire, he pokes the fire, he tears the wallpaper off the wall, a strip with shepherds on it comes down, he pulls the pendulum off the grandfather clock, and he rips up the fairy-tale book he's been reading.

(7) Then the fire leaps out of the fireplace and says, "You know, fires can warm people but they can burn very wicked boys! Burn! Burn! You are wretched and you shouldn't behave like this." The fire chases him around the room until, in the end, the ashes put out the fire.

(8) Little shepherds and shepherdesses come dancing off the wallpaper singing a very tender, sad song about how they were torn apart from each other when the little boy tore the wallpaper. They do a beautiful dance; the shepherds go off one way and the shepherdesses another with their pink sheep and blue trees, and the little boy is sad.

(5) Then he sits in the armchair that begins to move about and sing, *you wretched boy, you shouldn't behave like this. We'll be glad to see the back of you.* The *fauteuil* sings and does a dance with the little Louis XV chair, complaining about how wretched the boy is.

(6) When they have finished, the grandfather clock runs around the room singing, *"You wretched boy. Even I don't know the time now, so how can I tell it to anybody else? You are wicked and you shouldn't behave like this."*

(9) Then, suddenly, out of the book rises the golden-haired princess who says, *"You wretched boy! You have torn my book and now nobody knows whether I will live happily ever after. I feel sorry for you."* She is saying, you are wretched, but really I feel sorry for you. She sings a beautiful aria and all her anger and tenderness are in the music. Then she disappears into the book. And the little boy says he's fed up with books as well.

(10) Out of a lesson book jumps a noisy, crooked little schoolmaster character, Mr. Arithmetic, who starts rapidly reciting arithmetical problems, and also out of the book jump a lot of numbers. To the little boy's delight, the numbers run around shouting *5 times 4 is 36, 6 times 2 is 94,* and so on. The little boy is so thrilled with this, naturally, he runs around shouting all the wrong sums as well.

(11) Eventually all the little sums disappear and the boy is alone in the room with the black cat, which is now gigantic. Through the window it sees a huge white cat in the garden. The white cat starts singing to the black cat and their duet is not unlike the love duet of Tristan and Isolde.

(12) Then the black cat leads the boy into the garden and this marvelous music goes mad. The claustrophobic room disappears to reveal a beautiful, moonlit garden. "Oh, how marvelous it is to be back in the garden," the boy says. All the awful things that happened to him in the room have disappeared. He walks toward the huge tree in the center of the garden, but the tree says, "Oh, you wretched boy! You stuck a penknife in my side yesterday; you shouldn't have done that. The sap is still coming out. You shouldn't behave like that, you're absolutely wicked."

(13) Then a dragonfly comes up to him and says, "Oh, what a wretched boy. What you did to my sister! You took the beautiful wings of my sister and pinned them on the door—an awful thing to do." And then the squirrels and frogs come up and complain about how wretched the boy is, how naughty he is, how wicked he is. They complain so much and are so angry at the frightened little boy that they're all running around and one treads on the squirrel.

(14) When the boy sees the injured squirrel, a little compassion overcomes him. He takes off his neckerchief and ties up the squirrel's paw. All the animals watch and say, well, perhaps he's not too bad after all. They decide he is redeemable and, singing, "He is good, he is wise," they lead him to the great tree where, as the curtain comes down, he calls for his mother.

Designing Parade

Martin Friedman and David Hockney

As Hockney and John Dexter began working on the French triple bill they realized that strong measures would be required to unify the evening in the eyes of the audience. While it was important that the ballet and two operas retain their identities, they sought to relate them dramatically and visually. In Dexter's mind the three works were redolent of the atmosphere of World War I. Though Apollinaire had written *Les Mamelles de Tirésias* as a play in 1903, he rewrote it in 1917 as a strong anti-war statement and the young Francis Poulenc was in the audience for its premiere at a small theater in Montmartre, though the opera score was not composed until 1945. Also in the year 1917, Colette wrote the script for what would become Ravel's 1924 operatic gem, *L'Enfant et les Sortilèges*.

The problem was how to stress their spiritual and stylistic relationships in the Met's production. Hockney speculated about ways of using visual themes that would carry over from one work to another. Before addressing the issue seriously, however, he had to master the cavernous space of the opera house itself and understand its limitations as well as its possibilities. He began by making numerous drawings of the stage from every conceivable area of the auditorium—from the side aisles as well as the high tiers. Some were minimal, consisting of a few scrawls and notations, others were detailed renderings that took careful note of the curving balconies. After Glyndebourne, he found the Metropolitan auditorium to be somewhat intimidating; he wanted to know it thoroughly from the audience's view before deciding what to put behind its great curtain.

Obviously, the major difference between Glyndebourne and the Met is that at Glyndebourne everyone sees the stage in the same way—essentially as a flat front. At the Met, the stage floor has to be taken into consideration because so many people look down from the balconies. In fact, the best seats, I think, are those in the tiers. After I had taken on the job, I was told by some people that one shouldn't do the Ravel or the Poulenc in the Met space, because both operas are far too intimate for it. I disagreed. I felt you could do anything you

The Set for Parade 1980
oil on canvas
60 × 60

Glyndebourne Festival Opera House

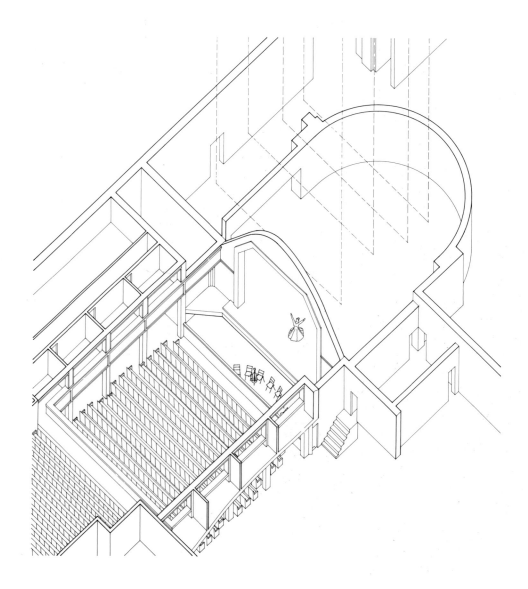

Bird's eye views of the Glyndebourne Festival Opera House
and the Metropolitan Opera House drawn at the same scale
demonstrate the radical shift required of Hockney when he
moved from the picture-book simplicity of the English country
theater into New York's most elaborate space for musical drama.

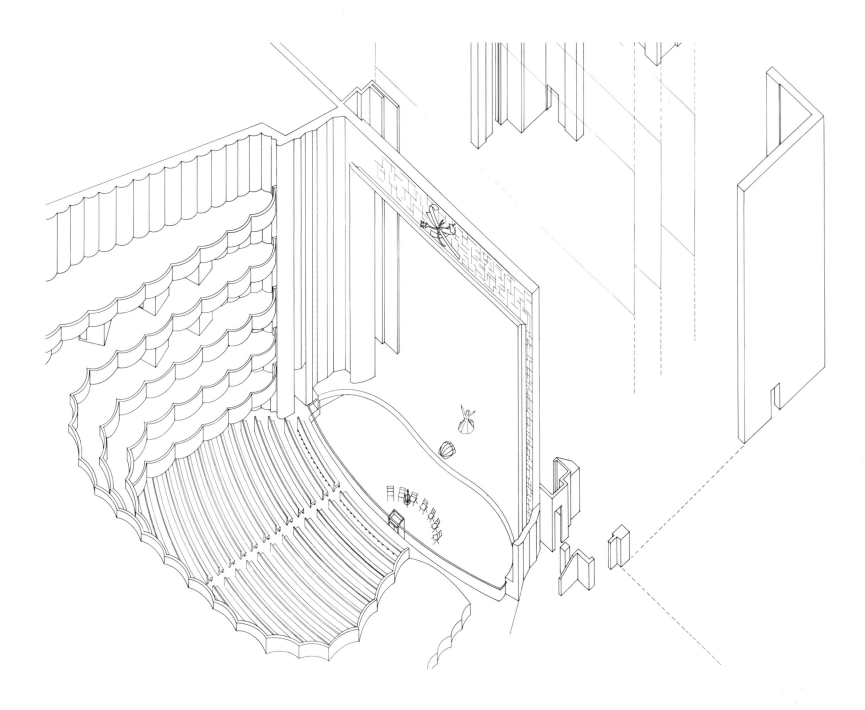

Giovanni Domenico Tiepolo
Punchinello Carried by his Friends 18th century
ink on paper
Collection Museum of Art, Rhode Island School of Design
Bequest of George P. Metcalf

wanted in that theater if you didn't think about its space in conventional ways. I must admit, though, every time I was away from the Met, it grew bigger whenever I thought about it.

Gathering up his stacks of sketches of the Met stage, Hockney returned to Los Angeles to think about designing the three events for its monumental space. Immediately, he constructed a cardboard model equipped with small figures. "Otherwise," he says, "you could never sense its scale." Next, he speculated about motifs to tie together the three productions. Taking a cue from the child's toys in *L'Enfant*, he came up with the idea of alphabet blocks to spell the composer's name at the beginning of each piece. By rotating and stacking the blocks, a few simple props could be created in an instant—notably the chairs, fireplace and giant stack of books in the Ravel opera. A second unifying idea was to have the blocks carried on and off the stage by the children's chorus in bottle-green punchinello attire, complete with ruffled collars, tall hats and masks. Hockney says the punchinello theme was suggested by John Dexter, who spotted a newspaper photograph of a Tiepolo drawing then on view at the Frick Collection and phoned Hockney in California to suggest "this might be our solution." Hockney took the hint and was overwhelmed by what he encountered at the Frick.

In that exhibition you looked at every single drawing—you scrutinized them. A show of 18th-century Italian drawings can be a bit boring sometimes—you look at some and skip two or three, then you look at something else. But this one was stunning. People have forgotten about such fine drawing. Not even Picasso could draw like that. Those Tiepolos have unbelievable, fantastic life. His technique was line with a wash to suggest volume, but the formula never bothers you because everything is so fresh. They're drawn in sepia, which makes them just that bit softer. When you see those drawings you realize that that particular skill has now disappeared.

Hockney was as taken with the wit and social content of the Tiepolo images as with their breathtaking facility. In the 18th-century Venetian artist's lusty world, the punchinellos were Everyman. Hockney decided to use these as characters throughout the Met production, an idea that made sense dramatically and stylistically, particularly since the *Parade* ballet takes place in a sideshow atmosphere. Also, there was the precedent of Picasso's use of commedia dell'arte figures in the 1917 production. For these reasons the punchinellos assumed increased importance in Hockney's conception of the triple bill.

I gave the Met wardrobe people the Tiepolo catalogue, pointing out that each punchinello was different. I said, "If you look closely, it's not a complete uniform. They all have the tall hat, every one wore a mask, but there are tall ones and little ones, fat and thin ones, chic and dowdy ones, babies—some with little potbellies."

He wanted punchinellos on stage in every possible variation. Not only would the soloists and the chorus of *L'Enfant et les Sortilèges* be dressed in

Punchinello's Masks
drawing for *Parade* 1980
ink on paper
22½ × 30

Villain
drawing for *Parade* 1980
crayon on paper
14 × 17

this mode, but so would the Met's stagehands who pushed and hauled the heavy objects that the little punchinellos couldn't deal with. Having those worldly veterans of Wagner, Verdi and Puccini so directly involved would require sensitive diplomacy, but Hockney can be as persuasive as he is creative. The stagehands, who are paid extra to wear costumes, do so with gusto.

Of the three productions, the ballet *Parade* had the most difficult beginning, and early in the planning it had been sandwiched between the Poulenc and Ravel operas as an entr'acte. Initially, Rudolf Nureyev was engaged to choreograph it, but soon it was apparent there would be no meeting of minds about its interpretation. There was ample precedent for such confusion, because even the Picasso-designed production in 1917 was a radical departure from the proto-surrealist narrative about a circus troupe that Cocteau had written. Once Picasso got his hands on the story, it became an instant vehicle for his invention, says Hockney approvingly, and he took whatever liberties with it that suited him.

By 1917, people were in such awe of Picasso that he could do whatever he felt like. He was a far stronger artist than Satie, Cocteau or Massine. I'm sure even Diaghilev knew that he was a very special kind of artist and whatever he did to alter the ballet, everyone had to go along with. Understandable.

Consequently, given *Parade*'s erratic history, Dexter and Hockney felt little obligation to follow the Cocteau scenario with its bewildering array of sideshow characters—the ringmaster, acrobats, the little American girl and a Chinese gentleman—and opted for a free-form approach. Basic differences in artistic viewpoint, plus his numerous performance commitments elsewhere, resulted in Nureyev's departure from the project. Though a few months later he was replaced by a new choreographer, Gray Veredon, the ballet design had to be put "on hold," with Hockney devoting his energies instead to the Poulenc and Ravel operas.

Though *Parade* was the last of the triple bill to be completed, it eventually became the curtain-raiser. It was Hockney's idea that its action introduce the rest of the program.

I suggested to John that we treat it as a little overture to what would follow. That seemed like a good idea, because in French, "parade" does not mean a parade. It means a sideshow with a barker in front of a curtain trying to get people into the theater—a very old technique that is still used in traveling theaters, carnivals and fairgrounds. That way, I thought, there were all sorts of things we could do with it. For instance, the typewriter that Satie uses in the ballet music suggested a scene with Colette typing the story of L'Enfant et les Sortilèges.

Though Hockney came up with many such original notions, the spirit of Picasso was looking over his shoulder. The hallowed first performance of *Parade* had to be dealt with in some way during the entire design process.

As to how I felt about taking on something which has become a sacred cow, Picasso's design, I decided to quote it, then forget about it. His curtain for

Parade *was a charming, traditional painting of a circus with harlequins, clowns, winged horse—everything; when it was raised, there was a cubistic city which the audience was supposed to be shocked by. I'd never thought of reconstructing the original* Parade. *As far as I'm concerned, there is no fixed work of art in the theater; every work has to be brought to life by the people doing it.*

Well before Hockney came into the picture, John Dexter wanted the triple bill introduced by an ominous battlefield scene, evocative of World War I. Hockney duly provided the coils of barbed wire, adding bright searchlights aimed into the audience. From the crowd of soldiers, one emerges and removes his gas mask and uniform to reveal the costume of the harlequin, the child's protector. The set undergoes rapid transformation to the carnival scene whose major element is an old-fashioned French music hall proscenium with a heavy red curtain. Because Satie's *Parade* begins with the famous "red-curtain music," says Hockney, this seemed the logical way to start things off.

It's a real curtain. Though I had drawn it flat, we made it up elaborately with bends, loops and folds. It could be pulled back for entrances. Above and behind the curtain was the suggestion of the big tree that would appear in the Ravel garden scene and some of the sky from the Poulenc opera. The idea was to have some of the characters in the ballet be those the audience would see later that evening. That way, we were getting back to the original idea—a parade before the curtain.

Thinking about the ballet, Hockney made innumerable drawings and gouaches based on the Picasso curtain, but finally decided to drop the idea in favor of the red curtain, a ubiquitous theme in his paintings since the early 1960s. His fantasy knew no bounds when it came to the costumes. In addition to the vivid attire of the little punchinellos, he invented outlandish costumes for the other performers. Among the memorable characters on stage were a gigantic female—played by a man—with an arresting set of polychrome breasts, one red, one blue, who was wheeled about in a baby carriage; a whirling ballerina in a French tricolor tutu; a pair of giant cats; the carnival barker; a scurrying waiter bearing a teapot and cup on a tray.

Hockney offered the audience a few tantalizing clues about what would follow. The top-hatted impresario, huge-bosomed lady and baby buggies foreshadowed *Les Mamelles*; the cats and the tea service would reappear in *L'Enfant*. However, because the ballet's action and decor were so kaleidoscopic, such connections were not readily apparent to the audience and, in retrospect, Hockney and Dexter felt they had overloaded it a bit with people and events.

I think a problem arose because too many characters were included. We did not need that many. After all, there was no story being told in the ballet. It was simply an introduction to all that would happen on the stage. Probably, very few people realized this at first. Perhaps some were aware of that by the end of the evening, once they linked it all together in their memories.

To rectify this, a number of sideshow characters were dropped in the December 1982 revival of *Parade*. Once the stage action was simplified, the

Curtain with Curved Stage
drawing for *Les Mamelles de Tirésias*   1980
crayon on paper
18¾ × 24

Zanzibar
drawing for *Les Mamelles de Tirésias*   1980
gouache, crayon on paper
18⅞ x 35¾
Collection Victoria Tenent,
Courtesy Andre Emmerich Gallery

association between the ballet and the rest of the evening's events were considerably clearer. But even with those changes, Hockney felt the brief ballet was not wholly successful, because what took place on stage did not truly reflect the introspective quality of Satie's music.

> *Cocteau wrote about a rather pathetic little troupe of actors who were not good enough to attract an audience for what was going on behind the curtain. There is a sadness in the music, and we couldn't deal with that. The music was pale and, in the end, you were probably looking at far too much on stage in relation to it.*

According to Joseph Clark, the Metropolitan Opera's technical director, even after Hockney delivered his models and gouaches to the staff, there were technical problems to be solved. "The specifics of how you would get from one opera to the next, how the surround of barbed wire would work within the context of the whole evening, and how the evening would fit together" had to be settled as the production took form. With Clark and his crew of wizards, Hockney and Dexter worked on the problems on a trial and error basis. It was a gradual process, Clark recalls, during which the technicians would fabricate various set elements, hoping these would do.

> *As John and David put the show together, we found out what was really required. Sometimes it was different from what we'd all assumed from the beginning—this system of working, though challenging, can put a bit of a strain on people. But it can also allow them to be a lot more flexible and creative, right up to the last minute. It's not locked into something that the director and designer might have decided two years before, without actually having had the benefit of a rehearsal.*
>
> *Fortunately, David was around all the time, so we could try half a dozen ways of doing something and asking, "Which one do you like? We think this one works, what do you think?" Usually he agreed. He rarely said no. Because the challenge was there, everyone had fun working on the production and he liked what we did.*

Les Mamelles, says Clark, was a perfect example of such collaborative problem-solving by the designer, director and technical staff.

> *The issue was to retain the simplicity of David's design, to move the elements fluidly into place and to light these effectively. What you see looks like very simple scenery on stage. You have an empty, dark stage, a show curtain, two portals and backdrop. But appearances are misleading; not visible are two special pipes hung with lighting equipment that illuminate the portals and the backdrop and an iron staircase that allows Thérèse to get to the second level window to address the audience. Now, all that scenery is flown in the air, and by the time it comes into view, you can't see the staircase and you can't see the lights. All you really see are three pieces of scenery. It's tricky.*

Les Mamelles de Tirésias (The Breasts of Tiresias) takes place in the hypothetical town of Zanzibar, somewhere along the Côte d'Azur. Its ironies were emphasized in the Dexter/Hockney production. The great gender

switch, in which the heretofore obedient wife, zealous to serve the Republic, takes on the attributes of a man, beard and all, while her hapless husband is relegated to the breeding and care of endless children, is the comic facade of this mordant tale.

As a narrative, Hockney points out, *Les Mamelles* makes little sense. To make its anti-war point, it blithely turns reality upside down.

It's an absurdist play. The plot doesn't really follow from one thing to another. It's full of mad events that together make up a kind of collage. Probably, Apollinaire was self-conscious about making what he thought was a cubist play. Poulenc said he "de-cubified" it. What that means, I do not know. The music certainly took a great deal from the French music hall.

Les Mamelles opens with a top-hatted master of ceremonies standing before an enormous fleur-de-lis curtain. Clark's crew translated this design from a small Hockney sketch executed in blue crayon over a pink crayon background. By incising a design into the blue overlay, the pink flower pattern was created. The drawing, Clark remembers, "had a little impasto, a certain kind of look, but trying to come up with that look on a large piece of scenery was again a trick. To match the drawing's quality," he says, "we used a piece of dyed blue velour, then in a sort of reverse process, the pink was put on with fairly heavy paint that built up the same kind of thickness. We got the same effect that David had achieved."

Once the master of ceremonies makes his departure, waving goodbye with an elegantly gloved hand as he disappears into the prompt box, the fleur-de-lis curtain is raised to reveal beautiful downtown Zanzibar. Hockney's design is at once confectionary and biting. Its sunny style recalls the lyrical Mediterranean vistas of early 20th-century French painting, those of Raoul Dufy in particular. Hockney has added a dash of Cubism in a few architectural forms that make up a plausible village square, complete with a striped awning and "tabac" sign. His ability to absorb and selectively employ diverse influences is especially apparent in the *Mamelles* sets. While he approximates the feeling of a Dufy vista, the large stage picture is also a wry commentary on the mindless tradition of "village square" art, with its well-worn clichés. Thus, Hockney's set is an affectionate bow to those innocents who for generations have painted nothing else but picturesque little vignettes. Under his fluent brush these all-but-exhausted forms suddenly assume amazing new vitality.

In *Les Mamelles*, Hockney has painted his village scenes on a series of backdrops, one in front of the other, using the same portal-within-portal design that characterizes the Glyndebourne *Magic Flute* sets.

I made two complete models for this, one much more cubist than the other. Then, John Dexter said he wanted to do it like an Edwardian review, basically in front of very simple drops. That's why we did it as three very simple drops with footlights. The characters' entrances and exits can be seen by the audience before they actually enter the set.

Cubistic Bar
drawing for *Les Mamelles de Tirésias*   1980
crayon on paper
18¾ x 24
Collection Steve Martin,
Courtesy Andre Emmerich Gallery

Punchinello with Babies
drawing for *Les Mamelles de Tirésias*   1980
gouache, collage on paper
14 × 17

Child with Shadow of Mother
drawing for *L'Enfant et les Sortilèges*   1980
gouache on paper
17 x 24
Private collection,
Courtesy Andre Emmerich Gallery

I thought the cubist model was better at first, but John said, no, the other one was much better for his purposes.

The most successful and stylistically consistent costumes for the French triple bill were those for *Les Mamelles*. Of course, the freewheeling nature of the script, with its liberated wife, victimized husband, amorous gendarme, newspaper vendor, newspaper reporter and fashionably attired populace, provided a wealth of opportunities. For the town ladies, Hockney alluded to the sculptural silhouettes of the early 20th-century French couturier, Paul Poiret and, as with the punchinello costumes, he provided the Met's wardrobe staff with an illustration of some authentic examples to be executed in patterned material of his own design.

The costumes for *Les Mamelles* abound in references to earlier Hockney work. The dashing gendarme, for example, was anticipated in a witty 1962 crayon drawing, *Colonial Governor*, and recalls the pompously gotten-up Polish army officers in *Ubu Roi*. He may be one of the few designers to have had the distinction of costuming two bearded ladies, the beguiling Baba the Turk in *The Rake's Progress* and *Les Mamelles*'s defiant Thérèse/Tirésias. As with the pulsatingly optical *Rake's Progress* designs, the costumes and set elements in *Les Mamelles* are stylistically of a piece. In fact, the vibrating patterns of the Poulenc opera costumes are virtually units of the set in motion, now merging with, now contrasting with, the boldly patterned background.

In preparing for the triple bill, the Metropolitan Opera's high command had wisely invited Manuel Rosenthal, the great interpreter of Ravel's music, to be the conductor. As a favorite student of composition of the eminent composer, Rosenthal knew how Ravel wanted his work to be presented on stage.

I began studying the work with Maurice Ravel at the precise moment L'Enfant et les Sortilèges was first done at Monte Carlo and later, when it was revived in 1926 at the Théâtre de l'Opéra-Comique in Paris. And I remember Ravel's bitter recriminations concerning the visual presentation of the work that was so dear to him. His unhappiness was so acute that he said over and over again he wished Walt Disney had illustrated his music, so badly had the designers and producers of the lyric theater served him!

Of the three works, the Ravel opera, *L'Enfant et les Sortilèges*, was musically the most compelling for Hockney. Listening to the music on his stereo and Sony Walkman, he identified as much with its composer as with its child hero.

From what I know of Ravel, I'm positive I would have loved the man. It's as though he were still alive. Manuel Rosenthal told me he was both sophisticated and childlike. Mind you, artists are often like that. The child in Picasso is obviously there—the capacity to delight in all kinds of things and to find the world constantly interesting. Colette's little story brought out the child in Ravel, which wasn't too difficult, and his music brought it out in me, which wasn't difficult either.

When they do L'Enfant *on the piano at rehearsals, you just don't get it. It's nice, but you don't get the color that comes from the full orchestra. I was deeply affected by it. When I first took it on, I didn't know the music well. I had heard it once before, but didn't realize how good it is. It's not childish, it's childlike. It's Ravel's music that makes* L'Enfant *great, not Colette's little words, although they're beautiful. If his music had not been so good, the story would be forgotten. The variety is stunning. He used forms of American music from fox-trots to bits of jazz. In the last scene, when the animals sing about how wise the child is, it's like a Monteverdi chant. It's like a collage, yet it's all Ravel. It has perfection about it—not one note too many, not one too few. I not only believe in the story, I believe in the music that tells it.*

Hockney's realization of *L'Enfant et les Sortilèges* was the French triple bill evening's most dramatic event. The little boy, to that point a passive witness to the ballet and *Les Mamelles*, becomes the central figure in *L'Enfant*. The child is replaced on stage by a young soprano. Like him, she is dressed in a blue and white sailor suit; her close-cropped hair completes the illusion. Working on the opera, Hockney tried to express the troubled vision of a child who, after a spate of unrepentant behavior is confronted by the creatures and objects he has so wickedly abused. From the outset Hockney wanted his designs to reflect the little boy's troubled fantasy. The interior of the Norman farmhouse and the ominous garden outside would be seen from this vantage. For its interior Hockney used exaggerated, hallucinatory perspective.

Painted on a huge drop was a great beamed ceiling that seemed to span the entire stage. The alphabet-block furniture was also large-scale, as a small child might perceive such objects. When the stern Mama asks the boy if he has finished his lessons, we see her enormous shadow on the slanted wall of his room. After a frenzy of destroying books, ripping wallpaper and other misdemeanors, the exhausted little demon falls asleep.

All that is enacted on stage has its musical counterpart at the sides. Flanking the proscenium are the soloists, dressed in punchinello and other commedia dell'arte costumes. Picturesquely deployed on randomly stacked alphabet blocks, each rises to sing a role mimed on stage.

Once the child has fallen asleep, the objects in the room angrily confront him with his misdeeds. At this point, Hockney's ingenuity is given full rein as vengeance in the nursery begins. The procession of shepherds and shepherdesses descends from the torn wallpaper, the fairy-tale princess tells her sad tale and out of the fireplace leaps a yellow-clad figure—a flame pursued by a gray ash. A wonderful pair of cats, one black, the other white, yowl at one another first in anger, then in passion. Through the bedroom window is seen a group of punchinellos seated under a great tree in the garden. They are the chorus, the voices of the animals and insects. As the backdrop of the room rises, the marvelous garden is revealed in all its luminous color. At its center is an enormous, red-trunked tree, the evening's most awesome image.

The Room
drawing for *L'Enfant et les Sortilèges*   1980
gouache on paper
22½ × 40

On the banks of the Nile, Luxor, Egypt 1977
black and white photograph

The garden in Part 2 of *L'Enfant et les Sortilèges*
as performed at the Metropolitan Opera House, 1982

The sources of the monumental tree, Hockney says, were many. Its basic shape came from a photograph he made in 1978 of two friends, Peter Schlesinger and Joe MacDonald, standing beneath a gigantic tree along the Nile. He says that in designing the opera, he tried to translate Ravel's music to color and line.

In fact, I drew the forms of the tree while listening to the garden music. When the cats finish their duet, the music goes mad, the room disappears and a great sweep of beautiful music fills the space. I drew directly on the cardboard model with a brush while listening to it. When I first began working on the garden, the trees were much smaller. At first I was thinking about a child in an intimate garden, but it suddenly dawned on me that in the child's view, everything should be gigantic.

Under the carefully controlled lighting that he and Gil Wechsler, the Met's lighting designer, devised, the color in *L'Enfant* took on palpable presence. It was dense and effulgent. The forms in the garden virtually pulsated under the colored light illumination.

I remember when I first showed my model to John Dexter, he said, "We'll light it directly with white light." But I said, "No, I've worked out more than that." When I said we should use blue and red lights on it I must admit he showed little interest, yet I felt that was how we were going to get visual equivalents of the music. He used to joke about "your colored lights" and I said, "Well, to my eye, it expresses the music."

172

When you see that color, with the blue light on the huge blue mass of the tree foliage, I think you physically take the color into your body as you take in the music. You can do this in theater in a way you can't do it in the cinema, because the cinema is not quite about color, it's about light. But where there's physical color, pigment, it's a different matter, isn't it? A physical color is a physical thrill.

Hockney worked out his production ideas for the French triple bill by using a complex, working model of the Metropolitan Opera stage. During this process he began giving impromptu performances of the opera for friends in his London studio. The model, an intricate one complete with fly gallery and miniature lighting system, had been sent to him by John Dexter. With this wonderful new toy Hockney began giving visitors to his studio a unique preview of what would happen in a few months on the Met's grand stage.

Never one to shrink before an audience, he took friendly drop-ins through the story animatedly. Once the lush Ravel tape was running, he was both commentator and performer, giving voice to the various roles in his unique *Sprechstimme*. He hummed along with the chorus and danced about while raising and lowering the painted flats. In his presentation of *L'Enfant* he was the incorrigible little boy, soon destined to see the error of his ways. For the lucky visitors, Hockney's one-man opera performances were superb show business. For Hockney, they were rapturous self-hypnosis. Word soon got out about these spontaneous events and a BBC crew found its way to his studio. Shortly thereafter a televised version of Hockney in action brightened the evening in thousands of English parlors and pubs.

In addition to using the elaborate stage model, Hockney made numerous gouache studies that fixed each scene of the three works in his memory and enabled him to think about transitions from one to the next. Indeed, much of the effectiveness of *L'Enfant* is attributable to the fluid movement of the set as the child's room dissolves into a vast, mysterious garden. This marvelous transformation, Hockney says, thrills the child.

He's left this room where everything had been nasty to him and thinks he's safe in the nice big garden—but of course things are still bad. I mean, the tree he carved initials into gets angry and the animals he had hurt earlier get angry. That's the moment in the music that is absolutely fantastic. At the first performance, you could feel the silence in the audience. Nobody moved. They, too, felt the way the child did. You shared the experience of the character on the stage, you really got into it—that's what made it work.

In this bizarre, dreamlike domain, the animals and insects are child-size. Perched on lily pads are the dragonflies, moths and bats who mournfully sing of the harm the child has inflicted on them and their brethren. Among the familiar creatures who accost him are a squirrel, a nightingale and a little owl, each with its own complaint. From the time he began working on *L'Enfant* Hockney visualized this climactic episode as a great panorama that would fill

(p 174)
Mr. Arithmetic
drawing for *L'Enfant et les Sortilèges*   1980
gouache on paper
14 x 17
Private collection,
Courtesy Andre Emmerich Gallery

(p 175)
Three Bats in the Garden
drawing for *L'Enfant et les Sortilèges*   1980
gouache on paper
14 × 17

173

the entire proscenium of the Metropolitan stage. It would be a moment of revelation. However, at an early rehearsal, the children portraying the animals were running about the garden.

When I saw that I was horrified. I said to John Dexter, "Keep them still; you don't need that movement. The color and the music will carry it together." We decided the scene should be static and that everyone should just stand still in the garden.

I always knew that moment would be magic. I knew, because I had looked at it so many times on my model.

Once the child redeems himself in the eyes of the garden creatures by tending the squirrel's wounded paw, there is a sudden mood change signaled by a musical surge and the great tree changes from ominous deep blue to vivid red.

This lyrical, highly original interpretation of Ravel's score was as stirring to its conductor, Manuel Rosenthal, as to the audience that experienced this remarkable fusion of color and music.

I regret with all my heart and all my attachment to my mentor that he was unable to see for himself the moving and brilliant collaboration of John Dexter and David Hockney at the Metropolitan Opera. The éclat, sharpness and mystery of his sets and costumes underscore Ravel's music. Hockney missed nothing: using the color red for the trees is an idea that marvelously illustrates the fantastic quality Ravel wanted to achieve in a garden populated by the child's numerous dreams. And the color and style of the shepherds' bucolic costumes beautifully conveys the simple way a child imagines a shepherd. Most designers previously charged with representing this work clad them, alas, in Louis XV costumes, like those one finds on 18th-century porcelain figurines.

Finally, fifty-six years after the opera's first unfortunate realization, Hockney and Dexter created a fairy-tale-like climate that would have enchanted the pure and passionate child that was such an important part of Maurice Ravel's life.

Child with Books, Cup and Teapot
drawing for *L'Enfant et les Sortilèges*   1980
gouache on paper
14 × 17

Le Sacre du Printemps

as told by David Hockney

Production series from *Le Sacre du Printemps*, as performed at the Metropolitan Opera House, 1981. (See Opera Chart, p 218) Chosen One: Linda Gelinas, Sage: Christopher Stocker, and the Metropolitan Opera Ballet.

(1) Stravinsky's 1913 masterpiece had a notorious premiere. His violently rhythmic, dissonant music and Nijinsky's wild choreography created vehement controversy and its first performance was one of the high water marks of early 20th-century modernism. (The performance shown here is the Metropolitan Opera's 1981 production, with sets and costumes by David Hockney.)

(2) Stravinsky's own description of that evening at the Théâtre des Champs-Élysées is entertaining: the conductor, Pierre Monteux, ". . . stood there, apparently impervious and as nerveless as a crocodile. Nijinsky, on a chair, shouted numbers to the dancers, which had nothing to do with the music."

(3) Only the set for Le Sacre seems to have escaped condemnation. Designed by the Russian painter Nicholas Roerich, it was recalled by Stravinsky as a "background of steppes and sky," apparently more descriptive than symbolic.

(4) In a 1920 Paris production, the Ballets Russes revived the work with choreography by Leonide Massine, in which the Chosen One was danced by Lydia Sokolova.

(5) In the current re-creation of Stravinsky's "solemn pagan rite," in which a young girl is sacrificed to the god of spring, John Dexter and I decided that the setting should be bleak and northern. In that decision we went back to the idea of the original production—an idea that other people had thrown out in favor of a more overt sexual treatment that featured near nudity. The young girl chosen for the ritual sacrifice is enfolded by a group of swirling dancers in a circle. Their faces are painted half dark and half light to suggest day and night. To the side stand the tribal elders who watch the adolescents in their feverish dance.

(6) The virgin disappears within the circle and emerges in the center of a great white cloth on which a large red spiral is painted to suggest blood. The colors on the huge disc behind the dancers, which looks like a stark northern landscape, go through a number of changes, blue at first and bright red at the time of sacrifice. In this wild process the dancers become a huge organism that renews itself through the ritual murder. These are basically primitive people, peasants in awe of the power of nature. In this ballet, winter will change suddenly to spring after the sacrifice.

Le Rossignol

as told by David Hockney

Production series from *Le Rossignol,* as performed at the
Metropolitan Opera House, 1981. (See Opera Chart,
p 218) Fisherman: Anthony Dowell (sung by Philip
Creech), Nightingale: Natalia Makarova (sung by
Gwendolyn Bradley), Emperor: Morley Meredith.

*(1) The opera takes place in ancient China and begins with a fisherman singing
about the beauty of the nightingale's song. Only he and a little servant girl who
works in the palace kitchen know about this wonderful bird.*

*(2) The emperor of China lives in a porcelain palace. Everything about the palace
is beautiful. The flowers in the garden have such a subtle perfume that little bells
are hung on them, just in case you don't notice. All the travelers who come to the
kingdom write about how beautiful the palace is. And the poets who come say the
most beautiful thing of all is the nightingale that sings by the seashore.*

(3) So the emperor, who only reads books in the palace—he doesn't go out of the palace—calls the chamberlain and asks why the most wonderful thing in his kingdom is something he does not know about. The emperor's court tries to find out about the nightingale—but the only one who knows about it is the little girl who washes dishes in the kitchen.

(4) They ask everybody in the palace, but the response is we never heard the nightingale—we don't know about it. Finally they find the little girl who says oh, yes, the nightingale that sings by the seashore is so beautiful. And they ask if she will take them to the nightingale. As a reward, they promise to make her Lady High Dishwasher and to give her the privilege of watching the emperor eat.

(7) So the nightingale sings for the emperor who is very, very pleased. In fact, the singing brings tears to his eyes and he offers jewels to the songbird. The nightingale says, "To a singer, the tears in your eyes are jewels. I do not need the jewels."

(8) Just at this moment three ambassadors from the emperor of Japan arrive with a present—a mechanical nightingale. It isn't a Sony or a Panasonic, it's old-fashioned clockwork. They open the box and wind it up and everybody's quite delighted. It sings away. Everyone thinks it's quite lovely, but it's actually garish and hideous compared to the real one. But they like it, and of course when it's wound up it always sings the same way.

(5) So she takes them to the seashore and on the way they suddenly hear noises and say, ah, that's the nightingale. And she says, no, no, that is a cow mooing. The nightingale doesn't sound like that. Then they hear another noise and say, ah, the nightingale, how beautiful it is! And she says, no, no, those are frogs croaking.

(6) Finally they get to the seashore and do hear the nightingale, but when they discover it's just a rather plain little bird in a tree, it's a bit disappointing. But they speak to the nightingale and ask, "Would you come and sing for the emperor?" And the bird replies, "Well, I do sing better by the seashore, but if you really want me to come, I will."

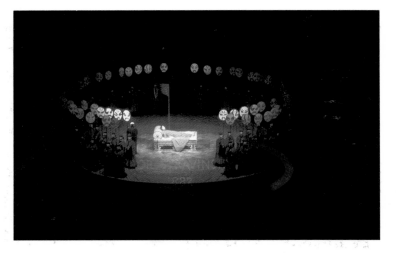

(9) The Chinese courtiers like what they hear and they think this new nightingale is probably less trouble than the little bird. So the real nightingale flies away. When the emperor realizes that the real one has left, he banishes it forever from the palace because they have a new nightingale. So he puts his toy on a post and every day it's wound up and it sings. But of course one day, in the middle of a song, it winds down.

(10) They can't repair it. So now there's no nightingale to sing and Death comes to visit the old emperor's bed and begins to take away the dying man's things: first his crown, then his sword of state, then his cloak.

(11) Just at that moment the real nightingale flies in through the window and begins to sing about the gardens. And even Death is charmed by the music and says, "Oh, please do not stop." But the nightingale says, "I'm going to stop. I will sing if you give back the crown and sword to the emperor."

(12) So Death gives them back and the nightingale sings more, then stops. Death pleads, "Please do not stop," but the nightingale says, "Give back the cloak to the emperor." And slowly, Death and all the ghosts from the past give back the things they've taken from the emperor. The grateful emperor then turns to the nightingale and says, "You can be the Lord High Singer in my court again. I want you to stay," but the little bird says, "No, it's better if I go away. I will come every night from the seashore to sing, and tell you about the beauties of your kingdom."

(13) All the courtiers, expecting to say farewell to their emperor in a room of darkness, are startled when they come back into his room. The emperor is sitting up in his bed and he greets them cheerfully. The room fills with light and everyone is amazed.

(14) At the end of the opera, the fisherman sings again, telling everyone to listen to the song of heaven in the voice of the nightingale. In the Stravinsky opera, of course, it's shortened a bit, but this is Hans Andersen's version of the story.

Oedipus Rex

as told by David Hockney

Production series from *Oedipus Rex*, as performed at the Metropolitan Opera House, 1981. (See Opera Chart, p 218) Narrator: Anthony Dowell, Oedipus: Richard Cassilly, Creon: Franz Mazura, Tiresias: John Macurdy, Jocasta: Tatiana Troyanos.

(1) When the lights go on, you see a narrator seated on a chair between the orchestra and the stage. He says this version of Oedipus the King will be sung in Latin and that he will tell the story in English as it goes along. As the music begins, a huge red circle emerges around which the protagonists are seated. They are Oedipus, his wife (and mother) Jocasta, his brother-in-law (and uncle), Creon, Tiresias the seer, a messenger and a shepherd.

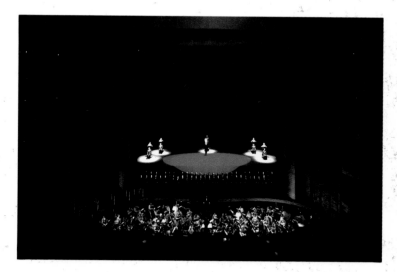

(2) A plague has descended on the city of Thebes and the people beg Oedipus, their king, to help get rid of it. But the narrator tells us that from the moment of his birth a snare has been laid for Oedipus: a hint of the tragedy to come.

(3) Creon returns from Delphi after consulting the oracle who has told him that the murderer of the former King of Thebes, Laius, lives in the city, unpunished, and that his presence is the cause of the plague. Oedipus assures them that with his skill in solving riddles he, the king, will find the murderer.

(4) The chorus invokes the gods and welcomes Tiresias, the blind soothsayer, with whom Oedipus consults. After some questioning, Tiresias reveals that the murderer of the king is a king. Oedipus is furious at these words and accuses Creon and Tiresias of treachery. Then the process of self-revelation begins.

(5) The men's raised voices offend Jocasta, and she says they should not argue in the plague striken city. "Oracles deceive," she says. Why, an oracle predicted that her late husband Laius would be killed by his own son, and yet he was murdered by thieves at the crossroads. This revelation horrifies Oedipus who explains to Jocasta that years ago on his way from Corinth to Thebes he had killed an old man where three roads meet.

(6) A messenger arrives to tell Oedipus that King Polybus has died and that Oedipus was not his real son but was adopted after he, the messenger, found him abandoned on a mountainside and brought him to a shepherd. Then the shepherd verifies the tale which has disturbed and frightened Jocasta. Oedipus thinks she is merely ashamed of his low birth, but the messenger and the shepherd make him aware of the fact that he had killed his own father and married his mother. Finally the narrator relates how Jocasta hanged herself and Oedipus gouges out his eyes with Jocasta's golden brooch. The chorus sadly bids farewell to the hapless king, bringing the tragedy to an end.

Designing Stravinsky

Martin Friedman and David Hockney

John Dexter's invitation to work on the Stravinsky triple bill proved irresistible to Hockney. His Glyndebourne experience with *The Rake's Progress* in 1975 had confirmed his devotion to the great modernist's music and, like Dexter, he considered Stravinsky's works for the stage to be rich in visual possibilities.

They were written as theater music, no matter how wonderful people say they are as concert pieces! Stravinsky meant them to be presented in the theater.

Early in the planning stages, the Metropolitan Opera had decided to produce the three Stravinsky works, *Le Sacre du Printemps*, *Le Rossignol* and *Oedipus Rex*, but then Dexter and James Levine, its music director and principal conductor, wondered whether the opera's corps de ballet should take on so heroic a challenge as *Sacre*. Though he and Dexter agreed on its great importance in Stravinsky's oeuvre, Levine explains,

. . . it was always given as a pièce de résistance instead of as a prelude, which is really what it is. Therefore, the weight of a big ballet was always resting on it. When you hear it in concert you wish there were some way to visualize it, but when you see it as a ballet you realize the music is much bigger. We thought, "We aren't a full-scale ballet company—how are we going to tackle this?" Then we shopped around trying to make other Stravinsky pieces fit in the slot, but for various practical and aesthetic reasons, nothing seemed right.

Hockney concurred, noting that the corps of dancers "does not have the primary mission of being a great company. Normally, they simply dance the slaves in *Aida* or the gypsies in *Carmen*. That's their job."

At one point Dexter suggested they substitute a work by Arnold Schoenberg, the 1924 monodrama, *Erwartung*, as part of the evening, because he thought this would offer an interesting contrast of works by two giants of 20th-century music. But even while this soul-searching was going on, Hockney and Dexter had begun working on what David assumed would, in the end, be an all-Stravinsky evening.

I didn't know the Schoenberg work they had in mind, but doing it didn't make

Raised Stage with Masks, Narrator and Auditorium drawing for *Oedipus Rex* 1981 gouache and tempera on paper 29 × 40

sense to me. At one stage the idea of another Stravinsky ballet, Pulcinella, even came up. I groaned. I couldn't get interested in that because we had used an awful lot of punchinellos in Parade. To begin the next triple bill with more punchinellos? I thought God, here we go again! Surely we could come up with something better.

During his first working session with Dexter at the director's house in New Jersey, they decided that the theme of ritual would prevail through all three Stravinsky pieces and Hockney considered various ways of symbolizing this notion.

I began drawing circles—simple little sketches, but always with circles in them. When we got back to New York, the Metropolitan still hadn't decided if there would be an all-Stravinsky program, so I asked, "Well, do I go ahead with my designs for it or not? You tell me."

Hockney's definite views helped persuade Dexter and Levine to return to their original idea of including Sacre, and once that was settled, there were animated discussions among the stage director, music director and designer about the shape and tone of the evening. During those trialogues, according to Levine, a strong argument was advanced for beginning the program with the ballet. "We thought we might have a chance with Sacre if it were a prelude to the evening, because a kind of shock effect would result from the éclat of the piece. With the fairy tale Rossignol in the middle and the monolithic Oedipus Rex at the end, the evening now really seemed representative of Stravinsky's theatrical variety."

In these early planning sessions, suggestions and strong opinions were tossed around with exhilarating abandon by the three men, and as Levine recalls:

I'm not sure if any of us could tell you exactly how an idea got started. Some of our original meetings were fast-going layers of responses to the music, to things we liked and didn't like in stage presentation, and to things we thought the house could do particularly well. There were even moments during our work on the Stravinsky triple bill when David would express something in musical terms, I would express something in directorial terms, John would express something in design terms. It was like three people fusing into a single creative unit, which almost never happens in such collaborations. Normally, one's functions and identity remain very separate.

Though the composer had left a number of ideas on the staging of his works, Hockney nevertheless wanted his designs to reflect the unique spirit of each.

The three works were distinctive, one from the other. Sacre was extremely kinetic, with dancers rushing around. Rossignol was more like conventional opera, with people moving about on stage. In contrast to both, Oedipus was a static narrative with music.

But the company's problems with Sacre were far from over, because, as in the French triple bill, the ballet proved to be the sticking point. Sacre, like

Set for Sacre with Dancers II
drawing for Le Sacre du Printemps 1981
gouache on paper
21 x 29½
Private collection
Courtesy Andre Emmerich Gallery

Primitive masks

Satie's *Parade*, was a modernist icon and the question was how to present it in new terms. And because the decision to program the ballet had been delayed for so long, it was late in the game when Jean-Pierre Bonnefous, a George Balanchine disciple, was finally selected to choreograph the piece. This delay left little opportunity for Hockney to collaborate with him effectively and he found himself operating in something of a vacuum, never sure how his design ideas would work with Bonnefous's conception of the ballet. Consequently, the design process was a prolonged one.

Parade and Sacre *took me longer to design than the operas, which is crazy. After all, a ballet set doesn't even take up the stage; you leave most of it bare for dancing.*

Some of Hockney's frustration while designing *Sacre* reflects his attitudes toward ballet design in general today. Unlike the early 20th-century productions of Serge Diaghilev, designed by such painters as Picasso, Matisse and Braque, those of such esteemed modernists as Balanchine are virtually without decor, the entire focus being on the dance itself.

Balanchine never cared that much about sets, because he didn't have to. For a great number of the New York City Ballet's productions, it's always been gray curtains or black curtains. Lincoln Kirstein told me that was his doing. He bluntly said he did not want abstract expressionists putting their work on the stage. That's what he said, and I was quite shocked, actually. There is no doubt that the New York City Ballet's tradition is an empty stage. Frankly, that's all right for a while, but personally I like theater a bit richer.

Various recordings of *Sacre* offered Hockney inspiration.

Somehow I remembered the music as being more pulsating than it actually is. A great deal of it seems to be an impressionistic description of a cold landscape. At times, it's almost like Debussy, and Stravinsky's own interpretation is among the most impressionistic.

Before Hockney and Dexter had decided that *Sacre* should be bleak and northern, David had explored other approaches. At one point, its fertility rite theme suggested the use of African masks and other tribal forms, but he soon abandoned that notion because such a setting was inconsistent with Stravinsky's ideas about the music. Its premiere performance at the Théâtre des Champs-Élysées in 1913 was given against a background of northern steppes, an atmosphere created by its designer, the Russian painter Nicholas Roerich. As Hockney says,

In our decision, we went back to the idea of the original production—an idea that other people had thrown out in favor of a more overt sexual treatment that featured near nudity. The ballet was about the dramatic change of seasons from desolate, bleak and empty-looking winter to the fullness of spring. That can only happen in northern countries. No, Stravinsky's music was not about a quiet, dear little springtime.

I did about twenty-five models for the Sacre set and I would light each one to see the effect of color on it, while playing the music again and again. When

Eskimo (Inuit) Mask   circa 1880
from St. Michael, Norton Sound, western Alaska
wood
7⅜
Collection Lowie Museum of Anthropology,
University of California, Berkeley

Primitive Masks
drawing for *Le Sacre du Printemps*   1981
gouache and crayon on paper
22½ × 30

197

I thought I had finished, I went off to a little spa in Germany, supposedly to relax, but I took the tape along and listened to it on my Sony Walkman. As I kept playing it, I realized my design wasn't quite right. In the end, I only stayed away four days because I found I couldn't really relax. I went back to London and worked on it some more, eventually getting something that was more satisfactory to my eye and ear.

The Metropolitan's opening night audience for the Stravinsky triple bill was greeted by an expansive drop curtain on which Stravinsky's name and birthdate were emblazoned in a large circle consisting of three color segments: green (for *Sacre*), blue for (*Rossignol*), and red (for *Oedipus*). The *Sacre* set was composed of two giant discs, one suspended, and the other on the floor, which gradually materialized through the curtain, which became transparent and then rose. Hockney intended these monumental circles to function symbolically, suggesting images of the earth and the cosmos.

The colors on the hanging disc were viridian green, cobalt blue, purple lake and ultramarine. By simply altering a few lights, we were able to change the whole mood. Under slightly blue light the suspended circle with the landscape painted on it went cold. Because the trees were deep purple, they turned a warm brown when red light was projected on the disc. The stage itself was earth-toned, and the blue circle on the floor could represent ice or a lake. Under yellow light it turned green and suggested vegetation.

Dancers in costumes of rough fabric that suggested pagan Russia circled the maiden who was about to be sacrificed. The painted faces of the dancers, their exotic attire and their frenetic movements were reminiscent of *Sacre's* melodramatic premiere in 1913.

In spirit, Hockney's designs for the fanciful *Rossignol* are more closely related to the French triple bill than to its companion pieces in the Stravinsky evening. Although it reflects the ceremonial character of ancient China, it is devoid of the weighty symbolism in *Sacre* and *Oedipus*. Instead, *Rossignol* is an elaborate fairy tale whose message is the superiority of nature's creations over man-made imitations, and of truth over artifice.

In Hockney's view, Stravinsky's shimmering music embodies the elegance and refinement of the Chinese emperor's court. The music's transparent quality brings to mind delicate porcelain glazes, a quality he sought to emulate in his designs.

You know, Stravinsky began the piece in 1909, before he wrote Firebird, *then abandoned it and didn't start writing on it again until 1913, after* Sacre. *Because of this vast stylistic gap, the* Rossignol *score sounds a bit disconnected. Another reason it sounds that way is you've gone from a simple scene at the seashore, with the fisherman (danced by Anthony Dowell) telling you about the nightingale's song, to the elaborate setting of the Chinese court with its bizarre antics. When that happens, the music suddenly goes from soft, undulating rhythms to harsh angles. I wanted to capture the jagged lines of the music, so it took quite a while to figure out how to represent the palace.*

Study for Costumes on the Stage
drawing for *Le Sacre du Printemps*   1981
gouache on paper
22½ × 30

199

Models for the silk drop (top) and the Chinese court in *Le Rossignol*, for the Metropolitan Opera, 1981.

(opposite)
Dawn with Orchestra
drawing for *Le Rossignol*   1981
crayon on paper
14 × 17

His research in chinoiserie inevitably led to the Victoria and Albert Museum.

I remembered those collections from my art school days and though I hadn't actually visited them for some fifteen years, I went straight to the gallery where they were installed and took about one hundred and fifty photographs. I really started scrutinizing those pieces, something I'd never done before. Of course, Chinese porcelain comes in all kinds of colors from different periods. The late 19th-century pieces seem excessive, like Victorian England, whereas earlier ones were more beautiful. I eventually settled on the early 18th-century blue-and-white pieces, because they were covered with wonderful representations of the sea, mountains and buildings.

Hockney painted directly and freely onto his cardboard set models, trying to capture the spirit of Chinese brushwork on the blue-and-white porcelain. The resulting design featured a large, elaborately decorated platter shape, which was the floor of the emperor's palace. In the Met production, this disc rested on a sharply raked stage painted black. Intersecting this circle was a tall, rectangular flat on which appeared a highly stylized representation of palace walls. In the scene outside the palace, distant mountains were suggested by cutout silhouettes placed behind one another on the tilted stage. In Hockney's later trip to China with Stephen Spender and Gregory Evans, he visited the Kui Lin Mountains, where he made numerous sketches and photographs. These unique natural formations could have been the source for Hockney's imaginary landscape in *Rossignol*.

Consistent with the tonality of the overall design, the emperor and his courtiers wore sumptuous blue-and-white robes and Hockney, possibly inspired by the elaborate makeup of the classical Chinese opera, adorned the faces of these lofty personages with abstract designs. Their attendants, the chorus, carried flat, painted masks on long poles. The masks' features were indicated by a few quickly brushed, curving lines; both sides of the lollipop shapes were painted, one with white brush strokes on a blue field, the other with blue marks on a white background. Despite the profusion of forms and textures on stage, Hockney kept his design monochromatic.

The only other colors you see are the red and gold costumes of the Japanese ambassadors who bring in the gaudy mechanical nightingale. Their flashy costumes were intended to make them look like the barbarians the Chinese considered them and all other foreigners to be.

Hockney also had a hand in programming the movement on stage. One challenge he and John Dexter faced was to devise an elaborate procession that would culminate in the arrival of the emperor. Though Stravinsky had provided some four minutes of music for this march, he left it up to those producing the opera to fill the time on stage as best they could. This would be a fine opportunity, Hockney thought, to emphasize the opulence of the Chinese court, and how better than with a parade featuring the fantastic

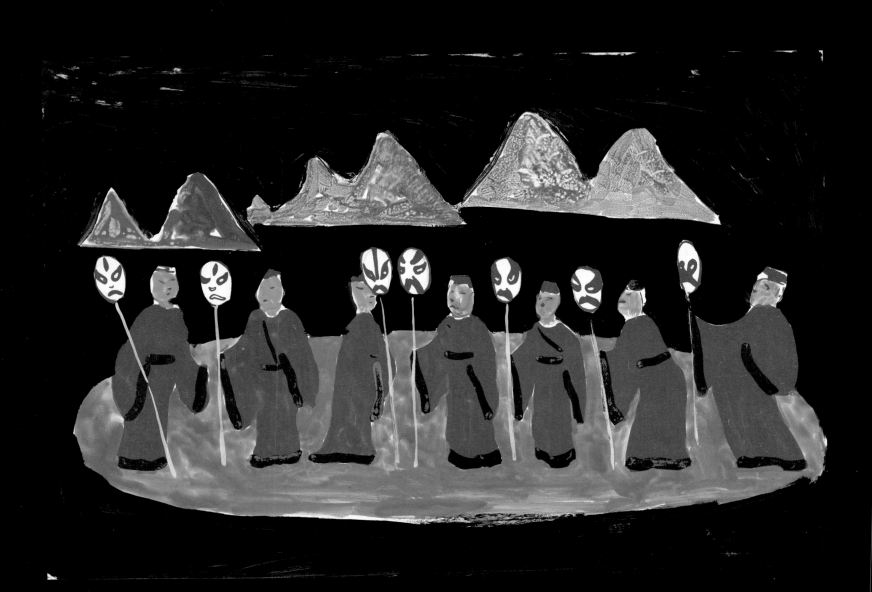

The book *Chinese Opera* and *Painted Face* was the source for the mask patterns in Hockney's *Le Rossignol*. In Chinese opera each mask represents a specific mood of one of the major character types.

Courtiers and Masks
drawing for *Le Rossignol*   1981
gouache on paper
20 × 29

animals that were part of the emperor's collection. He consulted books on Chinese history and painting.

I found examples of Chinese art in which people were carrying all sorts of things. I decided that our procession should include porcelain animals, porcelain flowers and two porcelain giraffes, among other things. I realize giraffes aren't Chinese animals but, after all, the emperor could have anything he wanted. In fact, I even found a picture of giraffes that had been sent to China. Also, elephants were sent to the emperor as gifts, but his people didn't know how to look after them and they died. Because dragons have special meaning in China, we decided to have a blue one in our procession. All the animals were carried around in a circle by attendants. We decided to use this occasion to show that the Chinese emperor's court was a very ceremonial place, and so it was easy to see why the people who lived there preferred the mechanical nightingale to the real one.

Based on his research Hockney made drawings of stone animals—lions, camels and dragon-headed creatures—from photographs of the Spirit Way of the Ming tombs. In transmuted form, some of these images found their way into *Rossignol's* procession.

In contrast to the richly attired mandarins, the true nightingale, danced by the elegant ballerina Natalia Makarova, was a subdued-looking creature in a gray-toned leotard. The costume Hockney provided was too bland for the dancer who asked him to embellish it a bit. He was glad to oblige.

I painted a few marks on it to suggest bird feathers, but she didn't need much more because she was so convincing on stage. Earlier, I had sketched costumes for the nightingale that included wings, but the choreography told me, no, the suggestion will be made through the dancer's movements—and it was. Makarova is unbelievably beautiful, and when she was lifted out of the tree, her arms fluttered like wings.

In its relentless gravity, the opera-oratorio *Oedipus Rex* was light years from the evanescent *Rossignol*, which had the elusive quality of a Chinese scroll. Of the three Stravinsky pieces, *Oedipus* was the most foreign to Hockney's sensibilities. Nevertheless, the artist, strongly attracted to its fateful story and powerful music, rose to the challenge.

I had a recording of Oedipus in London which I hadn't played for a long time. It has an amazing feeling of solidity—it's like granite. I had never seen it performed in the theater, only in a concert hall. My problem was to make one strong image fit this spoken drama.

Based on the Sophocles tragedy, *Oedipus Rex* at first seemed to offer few opportunities for Hockney to exercise his lyrical inventiveness. Virtually actionless, its plot is intoned by a seated narrator whose throne-like chair is raised slightly above the orchestra. On stage, the protagonists, who are seated on a dais, rise in turn to sing Cocteau's portentous words.

Consistent with the intent of Stravinsky and Cocteau, Hockney decided to emphasize *Oedipus*'s monolithic quality and to present it as a heroic tableau.

203

Roman architectural decorations at Herculaneum and Pompeii, as drawn by Giovanni Battista Casanova, circa 1760.

To heighten its ritualistic aspect, he expanded it beyond the confines of the Met's great stage, attempting to dissolve the boundaries between performers and audience. In fact, he determined to transform the Met house into a vast Greek theater and to make the entire auditorium part of the setting.

In his efforts to unite the stage and auditorium, Hockney thought in terms of a giant circle that would continue the sweep of the tiers in the curved backdrop. His initial designs also show two columns rather than a single one at rear stage and a row of masks on the curving walls. In the premiere production the curved background was retained, but the masks painted on it were too faintly defined for Hockney's taste, and he plans to strengthen these the next time the work is presented.

One of the biggest problems in designing *Oedipus* was where to place its large chorus. Among solutions considered was one reminiscent of Hockney's design for the Bedlam scene of *The Rake's Progress* in which the chorus would be "housed" in a giant, crate-like structure downstage and below the level of the protagonists. This was abandoned in favor of seating its members in front of the high dais from which the leads sang their roles. In effect, the final design formed a monumental staircase: the orchestra on the ground level, the narrator on the first step, then the chorus and finally the principals.

For all its monumental form, the *Oedipus* set was not a collection of heavy masses. Like all of Hockney's theater designs, it had a definite two-dimensional quality, as much the result of its stark, even lighting as its simple, frontal design. The music began in darkness, with a single spotlight focused on the narrator, Anthony Dowell. Suddenly, the whole stage was illuminated. In contrast to the dramatic coloration of *Sacre* and the hazy blue tonality of *Rossignol*, the lighting of *Oedipus* was intense and unvarying, the only addition being the circles of light projected on the ponderous white masks held over the singers' heads by immobile attendants.

I was constantly thinking about the Greek drama and the great space that actors and audiences shared in those old stone amphitheaters. They were so large that masks with various facial expressions were needed so everyone could see the actors from a distance. You always knew where you were—on stone steps looking at performers. Because the Metropolitan Opera House is made up of certain elements I couldn't alter—the proscenium and curving shape of the auditorium—I made them part of the design. Because I wanted to destroy the proscenium, I thought of the simple device of projecting lines of light on its sides so they would look like Greek columns. The shapes and colors on stage echoed what you saw in the auditorium; the large red circle on the dais was the color of the carpet; the chorus in black tie becomes part of the black and white pattern of the orchestra below it. On opening night, the audience was also in black tie, so everything blended and the whole theater was engulfed in the work.

In addition to Joseph Clark, who helped Hockney give large-scale form to his conceptions, the artist had the enthusiastic counsel of Gil Wechsler, the

Studies for Mechanical Nightingale
drawing for *Le Rossignol* 1981
gouache and tempera on paper
20 × 28

Study of Masks for Chorus
drawing for *Oedipus Rex* 1981
gouache on paper
23 × 29

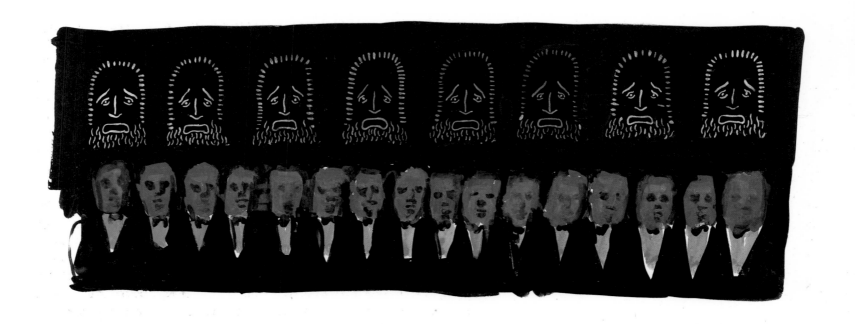

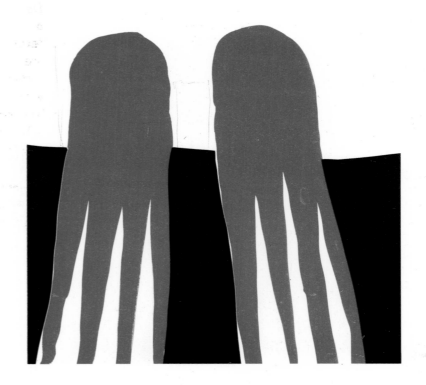

Chorus with Masks above their Heads
drawing for *Oedipus Rex*   1981
gouache and tempera on paper
11½ × 30

Blind Mask for Oedipus
drawing for *Oedipus Rex*   1981
gouache on paper
17 × 14

company's resident lighting designer. Because so much of Hockney's design was predicated on a fusion of color and light, it was necessary from the beginning to have some clear ideas about how these objectives would be realized. The artist had come a long way from the Glyndebourne experience in which the illumination of his painted sets was handled almost as an afterthought. Thanks to the elaborate model of the Met stage, coupled with its miniature lighting system, which was sent to his London studio by John Dexter, Hockney could build color changes into his designs. Because his work was essentially posteresque, depending more on painted illusion than actual volume much of its dynamism was achieved through the interaction of light and color. This was certainly true of the epic garden scene in *L'Enfant et les Sortilèges* in which the great red tree at center stage underwent extraordinary color metamorphoses as the opera's mood changed from menace to warmth; and it was certainly the case with *Sacre* in which startling seasonal changes were effected by colors projected on the huge landscape disc. The wizard of this alchemy was Gil Wechsler who, sympathetic to Hockney's desire to paint with light, came up with ingenious solutions that fully utilized the complex technology of the Met's lighting system.

For the Stravinsky production, Wechsler recalls, Hockney constantly fiddled with the intricate model of the Met stage, listening to the music and trying out lighting ideas. Hockney's approach to opera design was equal parts enthusiasm and innocence, and, as Wechsler puts it, he saw things on stage with a painter's eye.

> *David designed sets to be seen from edge to edge, like a painting, and created atmosphere with color rather than with other theatrical techniques, such as texture, light or shadow. . . David doesn't talk in theatrical terms—he doesn't use the jargon of the theater but always talks about the way he sees. He has a certain naiveté that never changes. That means he can always look at things with a fresh eye and doesn't lose sight of what he's set out to do.*

The images created by Hockney on the Met's stage, says Wechsler, have clearly affected opera audiences.

> *They're not used to looking at things on stage that way. The techniques that David has used are very old—paint on canvas and, aside from the props, flat scenery. But the way he's used color has been re-thought completely. It's as if David had said, "Okay, I don't want to think about the last 300 years. I'm doing this particular opera, how will I make it live on stage?"*

Last Act

Martin Friedman

When, in 1980, David Hockney agreed to collaborate with the Walker Art Center on preparing the exhibition *Hockney Paints the Stage,* his designs for *The Rake's Progress* and *The Magic Flute* for the Glyndebourne Festival Opera had already been widely acclaimed, and he had just begun working on *Parade,* the French triple bill for the Metropolitan Opera in New York. This is a faithful, if admittedly subjective, account of what actually transpired over the three years leading to the realization of the exhibition.

During our initial conversations Hockney and I speculated about a presentation that would consist primarily of sketches and models for opera productions he had designed, and about making museum-scale reconstructions of some of these. Our staff began tracking down sketches for sets, costumes and props, as well as models and photographs of performances. We discussed reproducing a few sets as faithfully as possible, but it was unclear how this would be done. In the world of theater, such tasks are turned over to skilled technicians who, working from sketches or small models, can duplicate every line and brushstroke of an artist's design with uncanny fidelity. Beyond recreating the sets was the question of how to animate them. Without actors moving about, Hockney observed, these tableaux could take on a leaden quality. During our various meetings I continually asked how he intended to resolve these issues, whereupon he would lapse into silence, his eyes taking on a faraway look. Sometimes, he would yawn audibly. I could take a hint—it was time to move on to another topic, or better yet, quit for the day.

Despite such vague responses, planning for the exhibition went ahead full speed. Because it was on the museum's schedule, we had little choice but to proceed on the premise that a number of set designs, scaled to fit our gallery spaces would, indeed, be built—somewhere, somehow, by someone. Hockney's assistant, David Graves, and I developed several schemes for placing these large, as yet unrealized, works in the galleries near costume sketches and set models for the respective productions. These spaces would also

David Hockney painting the garden installation for *L'Enfant et les Sortilèges,* Walker Art Center, 1983.

include early Hockney paintings whose themes and styles foreshadowed imagery and techniques that appear in the theater work.

At this stage in our proceedings—early for him, late for us—it was evident Hockney was still not fully focusing on what he had to do for the exhibition. In his view, it had not yet become an urgent matter. Besides, there were endless distractions: preparing and attending his exhibitions on both sides of the Atlantic, visiting Kyoto to look into Japanese handmade paper, making prints at Tyler Graphics, continuing his photo-collage experiments. Increasingly anxious inquiries were met with assurance that he was fully aware of what lay ahead and would give the matter his complete attention—after he had finished a few other projects. My doubts were not allayed.

Then, during a particularly frenetic work session at the Walker, the awful truth finally dawned on Hockney, and for a while his panic level matched mine. After a day or so of moody introspection he had the answer, and his face assumed a beatific expression. He, and he alone, would paint the sets. The task would be a huge one, he acknowledged, but definitely manageable. A major part of the work, he proclaimed, would be done in the new studio, which at that very moment was going up on the site of the unused paddle tennis court next to his house. Why not, he thought, inaugurate that space by painting the theater sets there? Its high ceiling and generous square footage would be ideal.

While the Walker staff was relieved that work on the set paintings would finally begin, the fact remained that seven large-scale environmental pieces were on the production schedule, and time was hardly on our side. Despite Hockney's willingness to take on such a gargantuan task, we felt that in the interests of time and logistics some preparatory work, such as construction of basic set elements, would have to be done at the museum.

We had already had a taste of what it was like to have Hockney working on the premises. During earlier visits he had turned the Art Center's board room into a disaster area as he spattered paint on hastily fabricated cardboard models. Stacked against the walls of this normally sanctified space were slabs of Gatorfoam, a lightweight, structurally stable material on which he drew with Magic Marker, paint and charcoal. In frenzies of creativity he would stretch across the conference table, leap over chairs, attacking, with paint-loaded brushes and handfuls of colored chalk, whatever white surface was available. It was now evident that some place other than the board room needed to be found for such goings on, so one of our galleries was temporarily converted into a workroom for the exhibition.

As soon as the Los Angeles studio was ready, Hockney was joined by a member of Walker's technical crew, Ron Elliott, whose expertise proved invaluable. An awesome supply of paints, brushes and great rolls of canvas arrived for the first project, Les Mamelles de Tirésias.

Meanwhile, back in the museum, the Walker division of the Hockney

A mask from the large-scale environment based on Hockney's design for the Bedlam scene of Stravinsky's opera *The Rake's Progress*, 1983.

workshop was going full force, as our crew, following the artist's directions, began constructing theater sets. Their first assignments were two scenes from *The Rake's Progress:* the auction scene, in which the exotic possessions of Tom Rakewell's wife, Baba the Turk, are sold off; and Bedlam, the opera's final episode, which features a cratelike structure filled with madmen. In the exhibition, these sets would be located at opposite corners of the gallery, with Hockney's small paper and cardboard models from the Glyndebourne production installed in cases nearby.

A highly skilled theater technician, James Bakkom, was brought in to duplicate some of the more complicated props. After extensive conversations with Hockney, using production photographs from Glyndebourne, Bakkom made remarkably accurate facsimiles of the crosshatched furniture Hockney had designed for *The Rake.* Before long, the mythological beasts from *The Magic Flute* also began to populate the temporary workshop, and soon, waist-high replicas of a teapot and teacup, and the grandfather clock from Ravel's *L'Enfant et les Sortilèges* were competing with these creatures for space.

Within a few weeks of beginning work in his Los Angeles studio, Hockney's excitement increased. He thoroughly enjoyed painting on so grand and lavish a scale, and as the colorful *Mamelles* set took form in brilliant reds, blues and yellows, he solved the problem of introducing "action" in witty fashion. Given the genial inanity of Poulenc's opera, in which husband and wife switch roles and do a little cross-dressing, Hockney's solution was right on the mark. A few years earlier in Paris, he had purchased dozens of small, stretched canvases in an art supply shop, simply because their diminutive scale and old-fashioned, handmade look appealed to him. Why not use them to create the opera's characters? In fact, *Les Mamelles's* personnae could consist of multiple parts; by switching them around, Hockney gleefully noted, all sorts of intriguing male and female combinations were possible. He approached this task with zest, painting sections of figures—heads, torsos, legs—on each canvas, which he placed, one over the other, in a manner reminiscent of the surrealist game of *cadavre exquis.*

After seeing that glowing manifestation during a visit to the California studio, I realized *Les Mamelles* was a breakthrough, but I also realized we were in for trouble in Minneapolis. Hockney had a new idea about how the sets should look and was moving away from merely duplicating the stage productions. It was apparent that the animals, teacups, and 18th-century furniture readied for him in Minneapolis were now simply too literal. It was only a matter of time before he would give us the word officially. We braced ourselves.

The Minneapolis crew was constructing the *Rake* sets according to Hockney's original dicta. The richly crosshatched boxes for Bedlam were done, and we were curious to know how he planned to represent the

211

madmen who would occupy them. We did not know that Hockney had already asked Ron Elliott to build a cardboard version of the Minneapolis set, so he could make the figures for it. He modeled each madman's head in Styrofoam coated with plaster of paris, forming fantastic visages which he defined with red and black paint. Some heads were adorned with pointed hats, some with beards, others with masks. Upon their arrival in Minneapolis, each head was mounted on a pole, around which an anonymous gray cloth was wrapped to suggest a body. From the outset, Hockney wanted some heads to be picked out with spotlights, an idea that was incorporated into the exhibition's installation.

Hockney's next big challenge was *The Magic Flute*, and an enormous canvas—forty feet long and ten feet high—was stapled to the studio wall. Using a gouache study made for Glyndebourne, Hockney began recreating Sarastro's sandy kingdom in tones of ochre, pink and green Liquitex. He especially relished using his long French brushes to define the Giottoesque rocks that frame the Egyptian desert. Unlike the roughly painted sets used in the theater, these panoramas would be seen at close range and therefore required the finish and detail associated with easel painting. So obsessed was Hockney with creating this heroic vista that he worked for long uninterrupted periods late into the night.

Once the huge background canvas was completed, the problem of breathing life into the *Flute* had to be faced. Instead of using the line-by-line copies of the Glyndebourne animals, which had been prepared for him in Minneapolis, Hockney decided to form them of flat, interlocking planes. The griffin and dragon were drawn on Gatorfoam, and their shapes were then cut out and fitted together.

It was increasingly obvious that Hockney's photography ideas were influencing the set paintings, and his photo-collage technique, in which figures and objects are fractured into numerous elements, inspired this new conception of the *Flute's* bestiary. In this idiosyncratic use of Cubism, the flute-playing Prince Tamino is a picaresque abstraction of multi-colored planes; and the dragon is a collection of feet, heads and tails. Walking by, the viewer observes changing configurations, and the animals seem to move.

By late September, Hockney and Ron Elliott had completed the major tasks they set themselves in Los Angeles. In addition to *Les Mamelles, The Magic Flute* and the madmen of Bedlam, they had finished two other projects: a lyrical evocation of *Le Rossignol* and a thirty-eight-foot-wide painting of the Norman farmhouse interior derived from Hockney's set for *L'Enfant et les Sortilèges*. Of all the set paintings Hockney made for the exhibition, *Rossignol* would prove the most abstract in relation to its stage version. Like *The Magic Flute* figures, its forms owe a great deal to his photography, which he describes as a means of freeing himself from the tyranny of perspective. By aiming his lens at various parts of a subject, he accumulates dozens of images, which are reassembled into a prismatic evocation of the original theme. Another influence on the design of *Rossignol* was his interest in Chinese scroll painting that began during a trip to China with Stephen Spender and Gregory Evans in 1981. The notion of a story being "unrolled" sequentially fascinated him, and he was also intrigued by the Chinese manner of representing space, which has little to do with scientific perspective. Figures and objects in the distance are not necessarily smaller. In this version of *Rossignol,* Hockney again carried forward the idea he had used in *Les Mamelles*—on a number of small canvases, he painted fragments of the story in watery blue tones. Recognizable in this mass of little rectangles are the interior and exterior of the emperor's palace, a procession of dignitaries, and the real and mechanical nightingales. Because Hockney wanted his new *Rossignol* seen against a dark setting, a large, black, velvet-lined enclosure was constructed at the museum, and not until the set's numerous components were fitted into their new home under soft blue floodlights, did he know if this interpretation would work. He needn't have been concerned, because in this atmospheric conception, his shimmering blue planes appear to float in infinite space.

Six weeks before the exhibition's opening, Hockney took up residence in Minneapolis in a borrowed apartment overlooking the Mississippi River, but little time was spent contemplating the view. At the museum, he set a fierce pace for himself and the crew. His job was to paint the theatrical environments our crew had constructed for him. The *Mamelles, Flute* and *L'Enfant* paintings, shipped from Los Angeles on giant drums, were unrolled and fastened to their respective walls, but despite such evidence of progress, there were fundamental challenges ahead. Hockney was still not certain how to deal with *The Rake's* auction scene, whose walls and furniture had been constructed to his exact drawings. After squinting at it for hours from various angles, he concluded it had to be changed—it was too faithful to the Glyndebourne set and lacked the vitality of the work he had just done in California. Our worst fears were realized, as chairs, sofas and Baba the Turk's what-not-shelf were eliminated from the room, and consigned to the basement to join James Bakkom's elegantly fashioned animals from *The Magic Flute*.

His next targets were the fastidiously crosshatched walls of Tom Rakewell's morning room, the setting for the auction scene. To heighten the chaos of the auction and suggest the disrepair of Tom's once elegant abode, Hockney assailed the walls with black paint and charcoal. On sheets of Gatorfoam, by now his favorite material, he rapidly drew outlines of alligators, Egyptian mummies and other memorabilia given to Baba by her noble admirers. Cut out by Elliott, these were suspended in profusion from the ceiling of the room. Using the same technique, Hockney and his assistant produced a crowd of 18th-century townspeople, basing them on Hogarthian prototypes. Some were simple silhouettes, others highly complex, richly modeled and multi-limbed. He crowded these optically scintillating, crosshatched characters

Hockney painting the walls of the large-scale work depicting the garden in *L'Enfant et les Sortilèges,* November 1983.

around Sellem the Auctioneer, whose flailing arms express the excitement of the bidding.

Still to be completed—with time rapidly running out—were two theater sets. For weeks a vast canvas reserved for *Le Sacre du Printemps* had stood as an accusing presence in the crowded workspace. Hockney seemed not to notice it as he walked by. One day, however, after finishing the auction scene, he showed up with an arsenal of brushes and plunged in. On its virgin surface he painted, in a highly expressionistic manner, a circle of elongated, primitivistic dancers. Above this frenzied scene, he suspended a large disc on which he described a bleak northern landscape in pale violets and greens, suggestive of trees and mountains. In the exhibition, both canvases were to be installed in a black enclosure, a slow-moving theatrical color wheel providing the necessary lighting. In his conception, the slow shift from blue to red would symbolize the transition from the deadness of winter to the regeneration of the earth in spring.

The theater set project the Walker staff was most apprehensive about was *L'Enfant et les Sortilèges,* Hockney's favorite work in the Met's French triple bill. In the Metropolitan Opera's production, the fusion of Ravel's sublime music and Hockney's radiant colors had a stunning effect on the audience, and he wanted visitors to his exhibition to have a similar experience as they walked into his new garden. The libretto is a cautionary tale by Colette, whose bratty anti-hero is cruel to animals and insects, rips the wallpaper, breaks the teapot and behaves abominably. After one of those tantrums he falls asleep, and in his dreams is led into a beautiful garden where he is upbraided by a host of creatures he has mistreated in real life—all this to the most exalted music imaginable, of course. Frightened, he regrets the error of his ways, finds forgiveness, and all ends happily.

The story posed difficult design problems in the exhibition as it had on stage—the major one being the transition from the child's room to the enchanted garden. On stage, the shift from house interior to garden was accomplished by raising an enormous painted flat. For the exhibition, the garden became a room dominated by a giant tree with a glowing red trunk. Hockney wanted visitors walking through the farmhouse door, into this magic, music-filled space, to share the child's sense of wonder.

The problems of constructing the garden were formidable. It had to be fabricated for easy assembly and dismantling, since the exhibition would travel to a number of museums in the United States, Mexico, Canada and England. Once the plywood walls of the room were in place, they were covered with canvas. To suggest grass, its floor was covered with newly purchased green carpeting. Using a scaffold pushed around the room by an assistant, Hockney sketched outlines of trees and clouds that he later filled in with pigment. His major weapon was a pushbroom dipped in a bucket of blue paint. Scrubbing happily away, he soon created a beautiful sky and spent more than a week

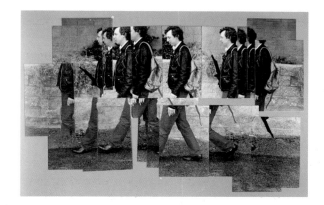

Gregory Walking, Venice, California, February 1983
photographic collage
12 x 23

blocking in the green hills, pink dragonflies, moths, frogs and bats on the horizon. During this time, he virtually lived in his walk-in painting and occasionally would be found sleeping behind a lily pad.

For all the effort that he put into Ravel's garden, as it came to be known at the Walker, not all went smoothly. Hockney had relied on theater technicians to help light his Eden, the idea being to intensify its painted surfaces by using colored gelatins on the spotlights—blue on the sky, green on the grass, red on the tree trunk. He wanted the color to pulsate, to be palpable as it was to the opera audience, but it was soon evident that lighting for the theater and for a museum exhibition have little in common. After a few frustrating days of experimentation, Hockney abandoned the high-tech equipment recommended by the consultants and with a few well-placed gallery lights, was able to achieve his objective.

Next, he turned his attention to the farmhouse interior from which the garden is entered. To suggest a small child's perception of the room, he rendered the ceiling beams in greatly exaggerated perspective. His method of representing furniture in the exhibition's room was similar to that he had employed in the Met production. The large alphabet blocks which introduced each work in the French triple bill by spelling the composers' names—Erik Satie, Francis Poulenc and Maurice Ravel—had other functions. Turned around and stacked in various configurations, these became furniture. For the Walker exhibition, parts of the fireplace and armchairs were painted on the sides of these cubes. A major character in Ravel's opera is the golden-haired princess in the fairy-tale book that was destroyed by the child. In the exhibition, she is ingeniously portrayed as a sequence of figures, each larger than the other, emerging from the pages of the book. The immediate source for this treatment is the 1982 photo-collage composed of a number of contiguous and overlapping images of Gregory Evans walking.

No one, least of all the artist, had any idea that *Hockney Paints the Stage* would become a vehicle for so much of his new work. Unwilling to simply reproduce past efforts, he used the exhibition as an opportunity to interpret earlier themes in new ways. In effect, the museum became a giant studio for his experimentation. Although the pressure of producing the exhibition on time increased daily, he had no hesitancy about discarding what he considered unsuccessful and beginning over again. The joy of painting on such a grand scale and enlivening these new sets with figures, animals and props, gave him enormous pleasure and he took as much time as he needed. While we may have experienced moments of panic, Hockney had no doubt about his ability to complete the work he had set out for himself, and as things turned out, Walker Art Center found itself commissioning him to create seven large-scale works that proved to be the most important elements of the exhibition. Our joint venture with the artist never lacked suspense or surprise. For everyone involved, it was an exhilarating journey into the unknown.

215

(overleaf, above and opposite)
Large-scale painted environment based on Hockney's
design for Poulenc's opera
Les Mamelles de Tirésias 1983
oil on canvas with separate elements
overall dimensions: 134 x 288 x 120
Collection Walker Art Center
Gift of the artist

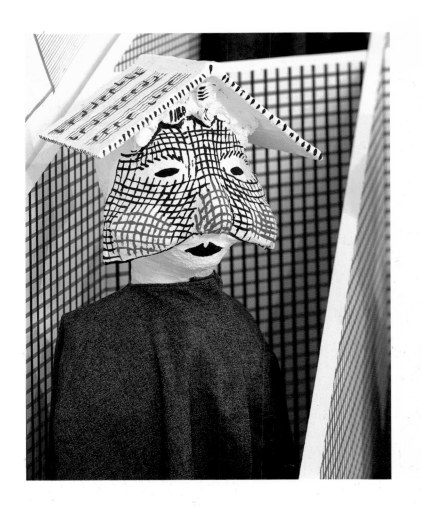 

(overleaf, above and opposite)
Large-scale painted environment based on Hockney's
design for the Bedlam scene from Stravinsky's opera
The Rake's Progress 1983
ink on canvas, acrylic on plaster, wood, cloth,
with separate elements
overall dimensions 120 x 192 x 192

(overleaf, above and opposite)
Large-scale painted environment based on Hockney's
design for Tom's Morning Room, Auction scene, for
Stravinsky's opera
The Rake's Progress   1983
ink, charcoal on canvas and laminated foam board with
separate elements.
overall dimensions: 120 x 192 x 192

227

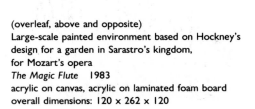

(overleaf, above and opposite)
Large-scale painted environment based on Hockney's
design for a garden in Sarastro's kingdom,
for Mozart's opera
The Magic Flute   1983
acrylic on canvas, acrylic on laminated foam board
overall dimensions: 120 x 262 x 120

230

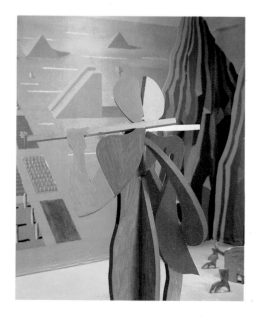

(overleaf, above and opposite)
Large-scale painted environment based on Hockney's
design for the room and the garden in Ravel's opera
L'Enfant et les Sortilèges 1983
acrylic on canvas, acrylic on wood, carpeting,
wool velour, colored light, with separate elements
overall dimensions: 155 x 457 x 350

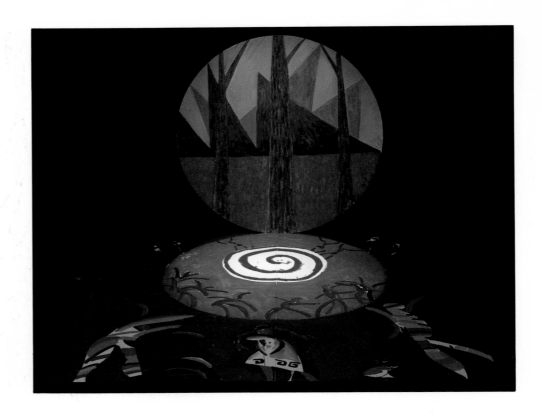

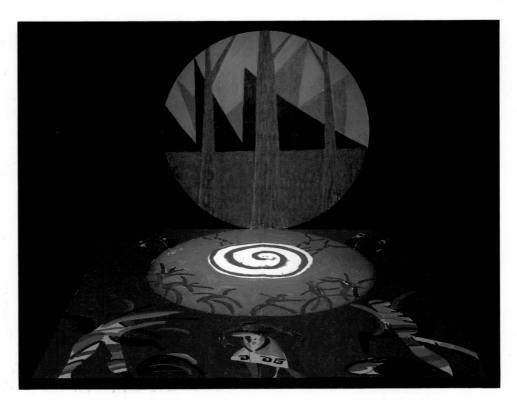

Lighting changes evoke the four seasons in this large-scale
painting based on Hockney's design for Stravinsky's ballet
Le Sacre du Printemps 1983
oil on canvas, colored light
overall dimensions: 144 x 180 x 180

236

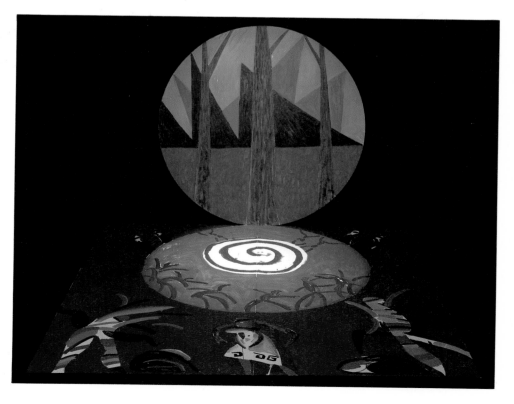

Walking past Le Rossignol

984   # 12   *David Hockney*

(overleaf)
Walking Past Le Rossignol, April 1984
photographic collage
36¾ x 73¼

Details from large-scale painting based on Hockney's
design for *Le Rossignol*   1983
oil on canvas, wood construction
overall dimensions: 144 x 312 x 120

Curtain Call

Hockney's work in painting, drawing, printmaking, photography and theater design is of a piece, but his periods of concentration in one area are usually occasions for developing ideas that carry over into others. When he takes on a project it can be all-consuming. Once the design of *Parade* began he was so preoccupied with its resolution that he could focus on little else. The same total immersion describes his work on the Stravinsky triple bill. However abrupt the shift from one medium to another, a commonality of form, color and attitude about space underlies all of Hockney's work.

Hockney is well past the point where theater design is an isolated aspect of his career. While filling a giant proscenium with changing images would seem at the other extreme from painting in the studio, in his case the same sensibility prevails. Not only do his two-dimensional ideas hold their own and translate admirably to the monumental public arena of the opera, but the process works in reverse. Images that evolve in his opera designs periodically surface in his paintings.

The invitations from Glyndebourne and the Metropolitan resulted in some of his most creative work. In both instances he was ready for new challenges. In each case it meant leaving the sanctuary of the studio where he had total control and subordinating his creative impulses to the requirements of a narrative with music. It meant an interaction with other strong egos, as knowledgeable about music and theater as he was about painting. It also meant frequent compromise and the realization that some designs work better on paper than on the stage. While he accepted these conditions readily, he by no means confined his contributions at Glyndebourne and the Metropolitan to costume and scenic design. While open to the suggestions of others for the look of a particular set element, he regarded himself as an equal partner in determining the overall spirit of a production.

Parade was especially important, because it offered him an opportunity to apply a spontaneous, painterly approach to theater design. The music's fantasy was expressed on stage in large areas of high-intensity hues. Similar

qualities characterize the vibrant California landscape paintings that followed *Parade*. The Stravinsky triple bill generated an entirely different fallout. This time, instead of continuing those images in paintings, Hockney took another tack. He became obsessed with making large, photomosaic compositions, consisting of figures in interiors and panoramic landscapes. Though these do not have direct associations with his theater sets, some relationship does exist. These faceted images, composed of dozens of overlapping Kodak prints, like his theater sets, are centralized and symmetrical. As in his theater designs, we are conscious of layers of flat planes that, cubist fashion, exist in indeterminate space. There is also a relationship between Hockney's systematic photo analysis of a subject and his compulsive academicism of the 1970s. Just how the hyper-realism of his current photography will affect his painting is far from clear. It could even have a reverse effect. Because making photographs might satisfy his craving for complex description, his painting could well move toward a greater informality.

Hockney's set designs are gigantic paintings with movable parts. His forms are a subtle fusion of innocence and wisdom; his line is fluent and effortless, but arriving at this appearance of insouciance can be a rocky process. He makes endless sketches and cardboard models, waxing enthusiastic about an idea one day and tossing it out the next. He thinks on paper, and in the middle of a conversation is quite apt to begin drawing, sometimes oblivious of the fact that someone across the table is waiting for an answer. He always travels with a heavy portmanteau stuffed with sketch pads, Japanese brushes, colored pencils and tubes of gouache, not to mention endless rolls of film. When he is tired of drawing, Hockney begins clicking away with his Pentax. Thus, well armed, he is ready for any eventuality.

Except for a simple set, designed for Sir Frederick Ashton's ballet *Varii Capricci* which had its New York debut at the Metropolitan Opera in the spring of 1983, and sets and costumes for W. H. Auden's *Paid on Both Sides*, which opened in New York on 12 May 1983, Hockney has for the present taken a leave from theater design but, given his passion for it, there is every possibility that he will desert the studio again for a few exhilarating months on the stage.

Hockney Biography

1937–57 Born in Bradford in Yorkshire, England on 9 July 1937. Studied at the Bradford School of Art from 1953–57.

1957–59 As a conscientious objector did hospital work instead of national service for two years.

1959–62 Studied at the Royal College of Art where the American painter Ron Kitaj and other founding members of the British Pop Art movement were classmates.

A large exhibition of work by Picasso at the Tate Gallery in London during the summer of 1960 made a tremendous impression on Hockney, particularly Picasso's brilliant draftsmanship and the scope of his inventions.

First visit to New York City in 1961. Upon return, began work on a series of etchings, *A Rake's Progress*, a metaphoric account of his experiences in New York.

Won the Guinness Award for Etching at *The Graven Image* exhibition at RBA Galleries, London; also awarded prize in John Moore's Liverpool exhibition in 1961. Awarded the Gold Medal upon graduation from the Royal College in 1962.

Work from the early 1960s characterized by interest in artifice and theatricality.

1963–68 Traveled to Egypt at the invitation of London's *Sunday Times*. First one-man exhibition of paintings at Kasmin Gallery, London, late in 1963. London's Alecto Gallery showed his etchings.

First trip to Los Angeles; began living there in January 1964. Began making photographs with a Polaroid camera and working with acrylic paints; paint surfaces become thinner and smoother. Fascination with southern California landscape reflected in work dating from the mid-1960s.

Taught at various American universities between 1964 and 1967: the University of Iowa, Iowa City; the University of Colorado, Boulder; the University of California, Los Angeles and Berkeley. Extensive travel in the U.S. and Europe.

One-man exhibition of prints at New York's Museum of Modern Art in 1964.

In 1965, one-man exhibition of paintings organized by the Kasmin Gallery; among group exhibitions, Hockney represented in *London: The New Scene* organized by Walker Art Center.

In 1966, five one-man exhibitions in Europe, including an exhibition of paintings at the Palais des Beaux-Arts, Brussels, and of drawings at the Stedelijk Museum, Amsterdam. Also in 1966, commissioned by London's Royal Court Theatre to design the production of Alfred Jarry's *Ubu Roi*.

Began painting large double-portraits, including *American Collectors (Fred and Marcia Weisman)* and *Christopher Isherwood and Don Bachardy* in 1968. With a good 35mm camera, increasingly made photographic studies as references for his paintings.

1969–74 One-man exhibitions of prints at Kasmin Gallery and paintings at Andre Emmerich Gallery, New York. One-man paintings and prints exhibition at Whitworth Art Gallery, Manchester, England. Started work on set of etchings illustrating *Six Fairy Tales from the Brothers Grimm*.

Seven one-man exhibitions in 1970, including a major retrospective *David Hockney: Paintings, Prints and Drawings 1960–70* at the Whitechapel Art Gallery, London, and an exhibition of paintings at Galerie Springer, Berlin.

Continued work on double-portraits; commuted between California and England. Jack Hazan began work on *A Bigger Splash*, a film about Hockney's life and work.

One-man exhibitions at Kasmin Gallery and Emmerich Gallery. Moved to Paris in September 1973 where he remained until November 1975. A major one-man exhibition of paintings and drawings, *David Hockney, Tableaux et Dessins*, organized by the Musée des Arts Décoratifs, Palais du Louvre, 1974, presented seminal Hockney works made between 1961 and 1974.

Worked with Aldo Crommelynck, Picasso's master printer, on a series of etchings in memory of Picasso, who died in 1973.

In 1974, invited by John Cox of the Glyndebourne Festival Opera in England to design costumes and sets for Stravinsky's *The Rake's Progress*.

Produced a backdrop for the Ballet de Marseilles's new Roland Petit ballet, *Septentrion,* staged in 1975 just before the premiere of *The Rake's Progress.* Invited to collaborate again with Glyndebourne on a 1978 production of Mozart's *The Magic Flute.*

1975–78 Nine one-man exhibitions of Hockney's prints and drawings held in 1975, including print retrospectives at the Gallery d'eendt, Amsterdam, Galerie Bleue, Stockholm, the Aalborg Museum, Denmark and exhibitions of prints and drawings at the Galerie Claude Bernard, Paris, and the Dorothy Rosenthal Gallery, Chicago.

In 1976, made a series of large-scale lithographs in Los Angeles which were portraits of friends. Began more extensive work with photography. Also in 1976, numerous one-man shows in Europe, Australia and the U.S. including a print retrospective at Louisiana Museum, Copenhagen, an exhibition of drawings at Nicholas Wilder Gallery, Los Angeles, an exhibition of prints at the Australian National Gallery, Melbourne, and an exhibition of drawings and prints at both Kasmin and Waddington galleries, London.

Between 1976 and 1977, made etchings inspired by Wallace Stevens's poem *The Man with the Blue Guitar*. Spent much of 1977 on designs for *The Magic Flute.*

In 1978, two major one-man exhibitions of Hockney's prints and drawings circulated in Europe and the U.S.: *David Hockney: Prints and Drawings* organized by the International Exhibitions Foundation, Washington, D.C.; and *David Hockney: Travels with Pen, Pencil and Ink*, organized by the Tate Gallery, London.

Work dating from the mid-1970s reflected a renewed absorption with invention and artifice, in part resulting from involvement in stage design.

1979–83 A retrospective of Hockney's complete print oeuvre, from 1954 to 1977, organized by the Midland Group Gallery in England in association with the Scottish Arts Council in 1979.

Commissioned by John Dexter of the Metropolitan Opera in New York to design sets and costumes for *Parade*, a triple bill with music by Satie, Poulenc and Ravel. Designed the Metropolitan's production of a Stravinsky triple bill the following season.

One-man exhibition of Hockney's *Paper Pools* at Emmerich Gallery, New York, and Knoedler Gallery, London, in 1980.

In May and June 1981, traveled to China with Stephen Spender and Gregory Evans. Also in 1981, drawings and paintings made for *Parade* shown at Emmerich Gallery.

Several exhibitions of photographs held in 1982, including *David Hockney Photographe* at the Centre Georges Pompidou which featured Hockney's large composite works, made up of many separate Polaroid photographs of a subject from multiple viewpoints and reflecting his long-time fascination with Cubism and Picasso.

Hockney continues to paint, make prints and photographs, and to collaborate on theatrical productions. Walker Art Center's exhibition *Hockney Paints the Stage* is the first comprehensive examination of the artist's work for the theater.

Selected Bibliography

Books

The Blue Guitar: etchings by David Hockney
who was inspired by Wallace Stevens
who was inspired by Pablo Picasso.
London: Petersburg Press, 1978.
Etchings by David Hockney, with text by Wallace Stevens, *The Man with the*
Blue Guitar. 20 etchings reproduced in color.

David Hockney by David Hockney.
London: Thames and Hudson, 1976;
New York: Harry N. Abrams, Inc., 1979.
A revealing and entertaining autobiography, with 434 illustrations and
lengthy text by the artist.

David Hockney, photographs.
London and New York: Petersburg Press, 1982.
Published in conjunction with a 1982 exhibition at Centre Georges
Pompidou.

David Hockney, 23 Lithographs 1978–80.
New York: Tyler Graphics Ltd., 1980.
Excellent reproduction quality.

18 Portraits by David Hockney.
Los Angeles: Gemini G.E.L., 1977.
Details of Hockney's large lithographs of 1976 are reproduced. No text.

Livingstone, Marco.
David Hockney.
New York: Holt, Rinehart and Winston, 1981.
Stylistic developments in Hockney's art are viewed in relation to sexuality,
literature, music, the theater and the history of painting.

A Rake's Progress.
London: Lion and Unicorn Press, 1967.
Etchings by Hockney.

72 Drawings by David Hockney, Chosen by the Artist.
New York: The Viking Press, 1971.
Reproduces ink and crayon drawings dating from 1963 to 1971. No text.

Six Fairy Tales from the Brothers Grimm.
London: Petersburg Press in association with Kasmin Gallery, 1970.
With etchings by Hockney.

Spender, Stephen and Hockney, David.
China Diary.
New York: Harry N. Abrams, Inc., 1982.
Spender and Hockney's account of a three-week trip to China taken
in the spring of 1981, with photographs, watercolors and crayon sketches
by Hockney.

Stangos, Nikos, ed.
Paper Pools.
New York: Harry N. Abrams, Inc., 1980.
Text describes how Hockney came upon the idea of the Paper Pool series.

Stangos, Nikos, ed.
Pictures by David Hockney.
London: Thames and Hudson, 1976 and 1979.
Based largely on *David Hockney by David Hockney.*

Catalogues

Baro, Gene.
David Hockney: Prints and Drawings.
Washington, D. C.: The International Exhibitions Foundation, 1978.

Brighton, Andrew.
David Hockney prints 1954–77.
Nottingham, England: Midland Group Gallery in association with the
Scottish Arts Council and Petersburg Press, 1979.
Full-page illustrations of the 218 prints published by Hockney up to the
beginning of 1977. This is the *catalogue raisonné* of Hockney's graphic work
to that date.

David Hockney: Drawings.
Minneapolis: Dayton's Gallery 12, 1974.

David Hockney: Travels with Pen, Pencil and Ink.
London: Petersburg Press, 1978.
A substantial catalogue produced to accompany an American touring
exhibition of Hockney's prints and drawings. Introduction by Edmund
Pillsbury.

Glazebrook, Mark.
David Hockney: Paintings, prints and drawings 1960–70.
London: Whitechapel Gallery, 1970.
Includes an interview with the artist.

Image in Process.
London: Grabowski Gallery, 1962.
Early group exhibition in which Hockney was represented.

Bowness, Alan and Friedman, Martin
London: The New Scene.
Minneapolis: Walker Art Center, 1965.
Group exhibition of British Pop artists in which Hockney participated.

Schneede, Uwe M.
Pop Art in England: Beginning of a New Figuration 1947–63.
Hamburg: Kunstverein Hamburg, 1976.
Hockney's early work is set in context.

Spender, Stephen and Restany, Pierre.
David Hockney, Tableaux et Dessins.
Paris: Musée des Arts Décoratifs, Palais du Louvre, 1974.
Text in French and English, including an interview with the artist.

Thompson, David.
The New Generation.
London: Whitechapel Gallery, 1964.
Early group show in which Hockney was represented.

Articles *Relates to Hockney's stage designs
Bailey, Anthony.
"Profiles: Special Effect."
The New Yorker, 30 July 1979, pp 35–69.

Baro, Gene.
"The British Scene: Hockney and Kitaj."
Arts Magazine, May–June 1964, pp 94–101.

Bowling, Frank.
"A Shift in Perspective."
Arts Magazine, Summer 1969, pp 24–27.

"David Hockney in conversation with R.B. Kitaj."
The New Review, January–February 1977, pp 75–77.

*Davis, Peter G. "Masks, Magic and Myths at The Met."
New York, 21 December 1981, p 71.

Geldzahler, Henry.
"Hockney Abroad: A Slide Show."
Art in America, February 1981, pp 126–41.

Gosling, Nigel.
"Things Exactly as They Are."
Horizon, November 1977, pp 46–51.

*Heyworth, Peter.
"Hockney's dazzling Flute."
The Observer (London), 4 July 1978.

*Hunt, Christopher.
"Progress, From A to The."
San Francisco Opera Magazine, Summer 1982, pp 28–33.

*Levin, Bernard.
"Hockney and The Magic Flute: will he next be called into The Ring?"
The Times (London), 14 July 1978.

*Mann, William.
"Hockney's Festival Flute in Full Flair."
The Times (London), 29 May 1978.

*McEwen, John.
"David Hockney Sets the Stage."
Portfolio, March–April 1981, pp 68–70.

Russell, John.
"David Hockney—A Storyteller Without Words."
The New York Times, Gallery View, 26 February 1978.

*————.
"The Spirit of 1917."
The New York Review of Books, 30 April 1981, pp 40–43.

Shapiro, David.
"David Hockney paints a Portrait."
Art News, May 1969, pp 28–31, 64–66.

*Smith, Philip.
"Sets and Costumes by David Hockney."
Arts Magazine, April 1981, pp 86–91.

Stadler, Peter.
"Elements of pop in *Rake's Progress.*"
The Daily Telegraph (London), 23 July 1975.

*Swan, Annalyn.
"The Rite of Stravinsky."
Newsweek, 14 December 1981, p 129.

Von Bonin, Wibke.
"Hockney's Graphic Art."
Arts Magazine, Summer 1969, pp 52–53.

Selected Opera Bibliography

Beaumont, Cyril W. *Ballet Design, Past and Present.* London and New York: Studio, 1946.

Buckle, Richard. *Diaghilev.* New York: Atheneum Pubs., 1979.

—————. *Nijinsky.* New York: Simon & Schuster, Inc., 1971.

Chailly, Jacques. *The Magic Flute, Masonic Opera.* (Trans. Herbert Weinstock) New York: Alfred A. Knopf, Inc., 1971.

Cooper, Douglas. *Picasso Theatre.* New York: Harry N. Abrams, Inc., 1968.

Cooper, Martin. *French Music. From the death of Berlioz to the death of Fauré.* London and New York: Oxford University Press, Inc., 1961.

Craft, Robert. *Stravinsky. Chronicle of a Friendship.* New York: Alfred A. Knopf, Inc., 1972.

Enciclopedia dello spettacolo. (11 vols.) Rome: Le Maschere/Unione Editoriale, 1954–68.

Gold, Arthur and Fizdale, Robert. *Misia.* New York: Alfred A. Knopf, Inc., 1980.

Lederman, Minna (ed.). *Stravinsky in the Theatre.* New York: Pellegrini & Cudahy, 1949.

Seroff, Victor I. *Ravel.* New York: Henry Holt, 1953.

Steegmuller, Francis. *Cocteau.* Boston: Little, Brown & Co., 1970.

Stravinsky, Vera and Craft, Robert. *Stravinsky in Pictures and Documents.* New York: Simon & Schuster, Inc., 1978.

Stravinsky, Igor (ed. and with commentaries by Robert Craft). *Selected Letters,* Vol. I. New York: Alfred A. Knopf, Inc., 1982.

Stravinsky, Igor and Craft, Robert. *Conversations with Igor Stravinsky.* Garden City, N.Y.: Doubleday & Co., Inc., 1959.

—————. *Memories and Commentaries.* Garden City, N.Y.: Doubleday & Co., Inc., 1960.

—————. *Expositions and Developments.* Garden City, N.Y.: Doubleday & Co., Inc., 1962.

—————. *Dialogues and a Diary.* Garden City, N.Y.: Doubleday & Co., Inc., 1963.

—————. *Themes and Episodes.* New York: Alfred A. Knopf, Inc., 1966.

Thompson, Kenneth. *A Dictionary of Twentieth-Century Composers (1911–1971).* New York: St. Martin's Press, Inc., 1973.

Wolff, Stéphane. *L'Opéra au Palais Garnier (1875–1962).* Paris: L'Entracte (the annals of the Paris Opera), 1962.

White, Eric Walter. *Stravinsky. The Composer and His Works.* Berkeley and Los Angeles: University of California Press, 1966.

Zenger, Maximilien and Deutsch, Otto Erich. *Mozart und seine Welt in zeitgenossischen Bildern* (Series X: Supplement vol. of the complete edition of Mozart's works). Cassel: Bärenreiter, 1961.

Selected Discography

Mozart, Wolfgang Amadeus.
Die Zauberflöte (The Magic Flute).
Lemnitz, Berger, Roswaenge, Hüsch, Strienz, Tessmer, et al. Berlin Philharmonic Orchestra and Chorus, cond. Sir Thomas Beecham (Seraphim LC-6129. 3 discs, mono.)
The one and only version! Although made in 1937, it remains a model of style. Unfortunately, it does not contain the dialogue. For more modern recordings in glittering sound, consult current catalogues. The Seraphim is a 1983 re-release, and has been excellently mastered and the surfaces are quiet (which was often not the case with earlier reissues of this classic recording).

Poulenc, Francis.
Les Mamelles de Tirésias.
Duval, Giraudeau, et al. Orchestra and Chorus of the Théâtre National de l'Opéra-Comique, cond. André Cluytens (Angel 35090. 1 disc, mono.)
The only recording of the work ever made. Although issued nearly thirty years ago, it is a definitive performance replete with Gallic wit. The original issue contains a handsome booklet with photographs of the first production, drawings by Erté, a short essay on Poulenc by Claude Rostand, a statement by the composer and a bilingual libretto with an English prose translation by Sherry Mangan.

Ravel, Maurice.
L'Enfant et les Sortilèges.
Wyner, Augér, Berbié, Langridge, Bastin, et al. London Symphony Orchestra and the Ambrosian Singers, cond. André Previn (Angel DS 37869. 1 disc, stereo/digital.)
Superb sound and a delightful performance. A 1961 recording conducted by Lorin Maazel on Deutsche Grammophon is also still available, but it cannot compare to the one listed here.

Satie, Erik.
Parade.
Royal Philharmonic Orchestra, cond. Philippe Entremont. (Columbia M 30294. 1 disc, stereo.)

Philharmonia Orchestra, cond. Igor Markevitch. (In *Homage to Diaghilev* album, Angel 3518 C. 3 discs, mono.)
The Angel album was issued in 1954 and is unfortunately out of print. It is, however, a document of the Ballets Russes and contains a sumptuously designed brochure printed by Mercure of Paris. The cover of this reproduces Picasso's drop curtain for the original production of *Parade*, and there are scores of black-and-white photographs, color plates and essays by Boris Kochno (Diaghilev's secretary) and balletomane par excellence, Cyril W. Beaumont. The conductor, the late Igor Markevitch, was Diaghilev's last protégé. The more recent Entremont album contains several other Satie scores, including *Relâche*.

Stravinsky, Igor.
Oedipus Rex.
Verett, Driscoll, Shirley, Gramm, Reardon, Watson, Colicos. Orchestra and Chorus of the Opera Society of Washington, D.C., cond. the composer. (In *Stravinsky: The Recorded Legacy* album, Columbia Masterworks LXS 36940, 31 discs, stereo.)

———.
Pears, Meyer, McIntyre, Dean, Ryland Davies, Luxon, McCowen. London Philharmonic Orchestra and John Alldis Choir, cond. Sir Georg Solti. (London 1168/5. 1 disc, stereo.)
The composer's own interpretation is authoritative and curiously cold-blooded, which suits the work. It is currently only available in a lavish album that gathers together all of his works recorded under his supervision. Issued to commemorate the Stravinsky centenary in 1982, this collection is a must for dedicated Stravinskians. The Solti disc is a brilliant one; Pears is outstanding in the title role, and Alec McCowen's narration is excellent.

———.
Le Rossignol.
Grist, Driscoll, Gramm, et al. Orchestra of the Opera Society of Washington, D.C., cond. the composer. (In *Stravinsky: The Recorded Legacy* album, Columbia Masterworks LXS 36940. 31 discs, stereo.)
The only recording available, and (at the present time of writing) only in the collection described above. The performance is sung in the original Russian and may be considered authoritative.

———.
The Rake's Progress.
Raskin, Sarfaty, Young, Garrard, Manning, Miller, Reardon, Tracy. Royal Philharmonic Orchestra and the Sadler's Wells Opera Chorus, cond. the composer (Columbia Masterworks M3S-710. 3 discs, stereo.)
This is the second recording of the opera; the first was made at the time of its American premiere at the Metropolitan in 1953 and utilized the Met forces. The present recording was made some twelve years or so later, and is far superior to the earlier set. The soloists are uniformly excellent, with Alexander Young outstanding in the title role, Judith Raskin a sweet Anne, and Rosina Sarfaty outrageously good as Baba. Unfortunately, John Reardon's Shadow cannot erase the memory of Mack Harrell's performance in the 1953 recording. The composer's conducting is lyrical. This performance is also available in the 31-disc album discussed above.

———.
Le Sacre du Printemps.
The Columbia Symphony Orchestra, cond. the composer. (Columbia Masterworks MS 6319, 1 disc, stereo.) Although there are nearly a dozen recordings available, many with spectacular digital sound, this is *the* version to obtain. It is made even more valuable by an introductory talk by the composer, *Apropos of "Le Sacre,"* which deals with the history of this musical landmark.

Opera Chart

	The Rake's Progress	The Magic Flute
Composer	Igor Stravinsky	Wolfgang Amadeus Mozart
Librettist	W. H. Auden/Chester Kallman	Emanuel Schikaneder/Carl Ludwig Gieseke
Premiere	11 September 1951 Teatro la Fenice, Venice	30 September 1791 Theater auf der Wieden, Vienna
Produced by	Venice Biennale, XIV International Festival of Contemporary Music, with La Scala, Milan	Emanuel Schikaneder
Conductor	Igor Stravinsky	Wolfgang Amadeus Mozart
Stage Director	Carl Ébert	Emanuel Schikaneder
Choreographer		
Sets and Costumes	Gianni Ratto	Nesslthaler
First Performance with Sets and Costumes by David Hockney	21 June 1975 Glyndebourne Festival Opera Lewes, East Sussex	28 May 1978 Glyndebourne Festival Opera
Conductor	Bernard Haitink	Andrew Davis
Stage Director	John Cox	John Cox
Choreographer		
Lighting	Robert Bryan	Robert Bryan

	Parade	Les Mamelles de Tirésias	L'Enfant et les Sortilèges
Composer	Erik Satie	Francis Poulenc	Maurice Ravel
Librettist	Jean Cocteau	Guillaume Apollinaire	Colette
Premiere	18 May 1917 Théâtre du Chatelet, Paris	3 June 1947 Salle Favart, Paris	21 March 1925 Théâtre du Casino, Monte Carlo
Produced by	Serge Diaghilev's Ballets Russes	Théâtre National de l'Opéra-Comique	Opéra de Monte Carlo
Conductor	Ernest Ansermet	Albert Wolff	Victor de Sabata
Stage Director	Leonide Massine	Max de Rieux	Raoul Gunsbourg
Choreographer	Leonide Massine		George Balanchine
Sets and Costumes	Pablo Picasso	Erté	Luchino Visconti
First Performance with Sets and Costumes by David Hockney	20 February 1981 Metropolitan Opera House New York	20 February 1981 Metropolitan Opera House	20 February 1981 Metropolitan Opera House
Conductor	Manuel Rosenthal	Manuel Rosenthal	Manuel Rosenthal
Stage Director	John Dexter	John Dexter	John Dexter
Choreographer	Gray Veredon	Stuart Sebastian	Stuart Sebastian
Lighting	Gil Wechsler	Gil Wechsler	Gil Wechsler

	Le Sacre du Printemps	**Le Rossignol**	**Oedipus Rex**
Composer	Igor Stravinsky	Igor Stravinsky	Igor Stravinsky
Librettist	Igor Stravinsky/Nicholas Roerich	Stepan Mitussov	Jean Cocteau
Premiere	29 May 1913 Théâtre des Champs-Élysées, Paris	26 May 1914 Théâtre National de l'Opera, Paris	30 May 1927 Théâtre Sarah Bernhardt, Paris
Produced by	Serge Diaghilev's Ballets Russes	Serge Diaghilev's Ballets Russes	Serge Diaghilev's Ballets Russes
Conductor	Pierre Monteux	Pierre Monteux	Igor Stravinsky
Stage Director	Vaslav Nijinsky	Alexander Sanine	(concert performance)
Choreographer	Vaslav Nijinsky	Boris Romanov	(concert performance)
Sets and Costumes	Nicholas Roerich	Alexandre Benois	(concert performance)
First Performance with Sets and Costumes by David Hockney	3 December 1981 Metropolitan Opera House	3 December 1981 Metropolitan Opera House	3 December 1981 Metropolitan Opera House
Conductor	James Levine	James Levine	James Levine
Stage Director	John Dexter	John Dexter	John Dexter
Choreographer	Jean-Pierre Bonnefous	Frederick Ashton	
Lighting	Gil Wechsler	Gil Wechsler	Gil Wechsler

252

Acknowledgments

In 1965 Walker Art Center presented an overview of recent English painting and sculpture called *London: The New Scene*. Among the young luminaries who came to see their work on exhibition was David Hockney who, since his graduation in 1962 from the Royal College of Art, had become something of a minor legend in the English art world. Recently, with his designs for the theater undertaken for the Glyndebourne Festival Opera and the Metropolitan Opera, his creativity has found vivid new expression.

It was another Hockney visit to Minneapolis that provided the idea for the exhibition, *Hockney Paints the Stage*. In 1980, the Walker Art Center presented works from the newly formed collection of the Musée Picasso, and it was David Hockney's great enthusiasm for Picasso's art that brought him to town. It was during his visit to Minneapolis that I learned about his new project, the design for the French triple bill, *Parade*, for the Metropolitan Opera Company.

Once Hockney began describing his ideas for the Met's stage, the next step was to discuss the possibility of an exhibition that would focus on his theater design. It was clear that the sets were a direct outgrowth of his paintings and therefore intrinsic to his artistic evolution. The proposed exhibition would not only bring together an extraordinary group of works in various media but also document the artist's creative process.

Once the exhibition's scope was defined, Hockney collaborated enthusiastically in its development, patiently enduring numerous interviews and participating in frequent planning sessions in Minneapolis, Los Angeles and New York. He approached the design of the exhibition as imaginatively as he would a project for the stage. Not only did he lend an important group of drawings, paintings and models from his own collection, but he made several large-scale paintings as part of the reconstructions of scenes from various opera productions.

As this exhibition took form, it was necessary to call upon the talents and knowledge of a number of individuals familiar with David Hockney's work. In Los Angeles we had the perceptive counsel of Gregory Evans in locating important drawings and paintings related to the theater designs. David Graves, who had assisted the artist with technical aspects of several of his theater set designs, helped us develop the exhibition's floor plan.

The New York and London offices of Petersburg Press were important sources of information on the locations of Hockney's works. Its director, Paul Cornwall-Jones, endorsed our project from the beginning and provided crucial

254

assistance. Christopher Burgess who manages the London office and Michael Bliss of the New York office provided valuable assistance.

Hockney has been represented by several distinguished galleries, here and abroad, whose directors responded positively to our requests for loans of works of art, photographs and documentary material. To John Kasmin, now of Knoedler/Kasmin Ltd., London, go special thanks. It was in his Bond Street gallery that I initially encountered Hockney's vivid paintings in the mid-1960s. Both Andre Emmerich and Nathan Kolodner of the Andre Emmerich Gallery in New York graciously aided with loans and documentary material.

Photographs and information related to both Glyndebourne productions were provided by Helen O'Neill, Public Relations. John Cox, in his capacity as Director of Production at Glyndebourne, invited Hockney to try his hand at *The Rake's Progress* and his insights about their collaboration appear in these pages. Also commenting in large measure on the Glyndebourne operas in this publication is the distinguished poet Stephen Spender whose perceptive essay deals with Hockney's ability to give visual form to myth and music.

The New York creative partnership of David Hockney and John Dexter at the Metropolitan Opera is also described in some detail. Dexter, in 1979, persuaded Hockney to take on the design of the French triple bill and, later, the all-Stravinsky evening. During a few candid sessions at a restaurant near the Met, the director spoke eloquently of how they evolved their concepts for both productions.

The Met's musical director, James Levine, took time from a busy rehearsal schedule to talk with me about the development of both opera projects at the Met. Another revealing impression was that of the eminent French maestro, Manuel Rosenthal, who conducted the French triple bill. His reactions to Hockney's visual interpretations of Ravel are particularly illuminating. Without the expertise of such indispensable people as Joseph Clark and Gil Wechsler, the Met's Technical Director and Lighting Designer respectively, Hockney's lyrical visions might not have been so fluently translated to the Met's great stage. Both men submitted generously to questions about working with the artist and it is a privilege to include their comments. For assistance in providing information related to the various operas and for providing the discography I am especially grateful to Michael Sonino. Philip Brunelle also kindly reviewed some of the text dealing with opera details.

So complex a project as this exhibition has involved the participation of many Walker Art Center staff members. It is a pleasure to acknowledge their important contributions.

I particularly want to thank the many individuals and museums who so generously responded to our requests to allow their Hockney works to be included in this exhibition. They helped make this exhibition a reality.

Martin Friedman, Director

Lenders to the Exhibition

Abrams Family Collection

The Art Institute of Chicago, Chicago, Illinois

Arts Council of Great Britain, London, England

Werner Boeninger

The British Council, London, England

John Cox

Andrew Crispo Gallery, New York, New York

Equinox Gallery, Vancouver, British Columbia

Mr. and Mrs. Miles Q. Fiterman

Mr. and Mrs. Richard Hedreen

Hirshhorn Museum and Sculpture Garden,
Smithsonian Institution,
Washington, D. C.

David Hockney

Mrs. K. Hockney

Indiana University Art Museum,
Bloomington, Indiana

Edwin Janss

J. Kasmin

Miriam and Erwin Kelen

Katherine Komaroff Goodman

Jean Léger

Sydney and Frances Lewis Foundation

Memorial Art Gallery of the University of Rochester,
Rochester, New York

Museum Boymans-van Beuningen, Rotterdam, The Netherlands

Museum Ludwig, Cologne, West Germany

Museum of Art, Carnegie Institute, Pittsburgh, Pennsylvania

Museum of Art, Rhode Island School of Design,
Providence, Rhode Island

The Museum of Modern Art, New York, New York

Nelson Gallery-Atkins Museum, Kansas City, Missouri

Galerie Alice Pauli, Lausanne, Switzerland

Mr. and Mrs. Morris S. Pynoos

Walker Art Center, Minneapolis, Minnesota

Washington University School of Medicine Library,
Rare Books Division, St. Louis, Missouri

Seven Private Collections

Reproduction Credits

All photographs not otherwise credited are courtesy David Hockney.

Courtesy Alinari-Scala: p 114 (bottom)
Courtesy Arts Council of Great Britain: p 41
Courtesy The Art Institute of Chicago: p 63 (bottom)
Courtesy Avery Architecture and Fine Arts Library, Columbia University: p 65
Ben Blackwell: cover
Courtesy The British Council: p 8
Courtesy Chang Pe-Chin: p 203
Courtesy Dance Collection, New York Public Library at Lincoln Center: p 129
Courtesy Andre Emmerich Gallery: cover, frontispiece, pp 6, 39, 42, 44, 46, 47, 49, 54, 122, 126, 128 (top), 131, 132, 156, 161, 162, 164–166, 168–170, 174, 175, 177
Guy Gravett: pp 62, 74, 80, 106–111, 120
Glenn Halvorson, courtesy Walker Art Center: dust jacket portrait of David Hockney
Huebner/Perna: p 215
Clay Humphrey: pp 90–97, 142–155, 172, 178–191
Courtesy Henry E. Huntington Library: pp 63 (top), 85
Courtesy Knoedler Gallery, London: p 22 (top)
Peter Langan: p 64
Courtesy Lowie Museum of Anthropology, University of California, Berkeley: p 197
Courtesy Metropolitan Museum of Art: p 115 (bottom)
Herbert Migdoll, courtesy The Joffrey Ballet: pp 38, 128 (bottom)
Courtesy Museum of Art, Rhode Island School of Design: p 160
Courtesy Museum Ludwig, Cologne: p 51
Courtesy The Museum of Modern Art, New York: pp 13, 76, 98
Courtesy National Gallery, London: p 114 (top)
Courtesy Nishimura Gallery, Tokyo: p 50
Courtesy Petersburg Press: pp 10, 14, (bottom), 20, 22 (bottom), 24, 26, 33, 36, 41, 57, 60, 69, 70–72, 86, 101, 104, 112, 134, 136, 139, 140, 195, 196, 198, 200, 202, 205, 206
Courtesy Staatliche Museen, Berlin: p 115 (top)
Lee Stalsworth, courtesy Hirshhorn Museum, Smithsonian Institution: pp 14 (top), 40
Courtesy Tate Gallery, London: p 31
John Tennant, Courtesy Hirshhorn Museum, Smithsonian Institution: p 28
Rodney Todd-White & Son, courtesy Waddington Galleries, London: p 27
Courtesy Tyler Graphics, Ltd.: p 52
Walker Art Center: pp 6, 34, 56, 57, 66, 67, 79, 82–84, 100, 103, 105, 116, 118, 208, 211, 212, 214, 216–241, 253

Walker Art Center Staff for the Exhibition

Administration	Donald C. Borrman
Registration and Shipping	Carolyn Clark DeCato
Publication Supervision and Editing	Mildred Friedman
Publication Design	Robert Jensen
Exhibition Assistance	Elizabeth Armstrong Marie Cieri* Trent Myers*
Editorial Assistance	Susan Higgins
Publication Index	William Horrigan
Tape Transcription	Susan Bloom
Public Relations	Mary Abbe Martin
Slide Tape Production	Charles Helm Jana Freiband
Photography	Glenn Halvorson Donald Neal
Set Reconstructions	Ron Elliott James R. Bakkom**
Installation	Hugh Jacobson Mary Cutshall Steve Ecklund Joe Janson Mark Kramer David Lee Cody Riddle Peter Schwob
Director of the Exhibition	Martin Friedman

*former staff members
**consultant

Index

Page numbers in bold-face type indicate illustrations. Hockney's works are listed alphabetically after his name. Hockney's works for the opera are cross-referenced under the title of each opera and are listed sequentially.

Travel Schedule

Walker Art Center
Minneapolis, Minnesota
20 November 1983 to 22 January 1984

Museo Tamayo
Mexico, D. F.
19 February to 15 April 1984

Art Gallery of Ontario
Toronto, Canada
9 June to 12 August 1984

Museum of Contemporary Art
Chicago, Illinois
16 September to 11 November 1984

The Fort Worth Art Museum
Fort Worth, Texas
16 December 1984 to 17 February 1985

San Francisco Museum of Art
San Francisco, California
24 March to 26 May 1985

Hayward Gallery
London, England
1 August to 29 September 1985